W0037853

Elite • 259

The Athenian Army 507–322 BC

NICHOLAS SEKUNDA

ILLUSTRATED BY GIUSEPPE RAVA
Series editors Martin Windrow & Nick Reynolds

OSPREY PUBLISHING
Bloomsbury Publishing Plc
Kemp House, Chawley Park, Cumnor Hill, Oxford OX2 9PH, UK
29 Earlsfort Terrace, Dublin 2, Ireland
1385 Broadway, 5th Floor, New York, NY 10018, USA
E-mail: info@ospreypublishing.com
www.ospreypublishing.com

OSPREY is a trademark of Osprey Publishing Ltd

First published in Great Britain in 2025

© Osprey Publishing Ltd, 2025

All rights reserved. No part of this publication may be reproduced or transmitted in any form or by any means, electronic or mechanical, including photocopying, recording, or any information storage or retrieval system, without prior permission in writing from the publishers.

A catalogue record for this book is available from the British Library.

ISBN: PB 9781472862808; eBook 9781472862815;
ePDF 9781472862822; XML 9781472862839

25 26 27 28 29   10 9 8 7 6 5 4 3 2 1

Index by Rob Munro
Typeset by PDQ Digital Media Solutions, Bungay, UK
Printed by Repro India Ltd.

Osprey Publishing supports the Woodland Trust, the UK's leading woodland conservation charity.

To find out more about our authors and books visit **www.ospreypublishing.com**. Here you will find extracts, author interviews, details of forthcoming events and the option to sign up for our newsletter.

Acknowledgements

I would like to record my gratitude to all who have helped me with photographs, Drs Wojciech Brillowski, Dorota Sakowicz and Bartosz Buszman, and to Natalia Kozłowska for supplying me with her excellent drawings. Work on this book would not have been possible at all without the grant of research leave by the Dean of Historical Studies at Gdańsk University, Dr Arkadiusz Janicki.

Author's note

Unless otherwise noted, all dates in the text are BC. The Athenian month was lunar, so the calendar required intercalation periodically. The Athenian year began on the first day of the month Hecatombaion, which falls within the modern months of June or July, when the archon, the chief magistrate, took up office. Hence the dates referred to in this book equate to two modern years unless we can date the given event more precisely. The annual archonship begins in 682/81 with Creon, the first archon to give his name to the Athenian year.

Front-cover photograph: Warriors and a chariot on the base for a funerary *kouros*, *c.*510, displayed in Athens (National Museum 3477). It seems that after the democratic reforms of Cleisthenes, statues like this, celebrating the athletic, military and other achievements of high-status Athenian individuals, were banned. (Dorieo/Wikimedia/CC BY-SA 4.0)

Title-page illustration: Upper part of a stele recording the ephebic oath, taken for the first time by the Greek forces before the battle of Plataea, from the sanctuary of Ares in Acharnae. The letterforms date the stele to sometime in the 4th century when Dion, son of Dion of Acharnae held the joint priesthood of Ares and Athena Areia, which cannot be dated more closely. In the tympanum is shown the defensive armour of a hoplite, including the muscle-cuirass introduced in the 360s. Note the Corinthian helmet. The object to the right of the muscle-cuirass is probably the folded cloak of an *ephēbos*. (© École française d'Athènes 12.300)

Artist's note

Readers may care to note that the original paintings from which the colour plates in this book were prepared are available for private sale. All reproduction copyright whatsoever is retained by the publishers. All enquiries should be addressed to:

info@g-rava.it

The publishers regret that they can enter into no correspondence upon this matter.

Chronology

CONTENTS

THE ATHENIAN ARMY 507–322 BC

INTRODUCTION

We probably know more about ancient Athens than any other ancient society thanks largely to the texts that have survived. Pride of place goes to the *Athēniaōn Politeia*, or *AP* for short, preserved on papyri bought by museums in Berlin and London and only published at the very end of the 19th century. The habit of inscribing public documents on stone, ever increasing over the 5th and 4th centuries, has done much to confirm and correct the picture derived from the texts. Attica is covered by volumes i and ii of the series *Inscriptiones Graecae*, which started in 1873. The volumes of this series are now in their second (e.g. *IG* ii²), and in some cases their third (e.g. *IG* i³) edition. For the student of warfare, however, the material evidence, both surviving military impedimenta and representations of armed individuals, is as important as the textual evidence. We are fortunate in the case of Athens to have this in abundance.

This book is concerned with Athens when it had a democratic government from 507 until its defeat at the hands of the Macedonians in the Lamian War of 323–322, over which time the military institutions of the state, though constantly evolving, remained largely unchanged. For the first part of this period, we have at our disposal Attic painted vases, which peter out when we enter the 4th century, but their place is taken up by funerary sculpture. This was banned by sumptuary legislation brought in under the regime of Demetrius of Phaleron (r. 317–307). The book is also concerned with the land army, rather than naval forces, although the fleet was manned by the same citizens who fought on land.

Athens might have had a democratic form of government over this period, but it is important to bear in mind that Athenian society was a slave-owning society; its economy was based on slavery. Consequently, its citizens could be released to perform military service without the economy collapsing.

The amount of modern literature dealing with the Athenian army is large, and in this book I have restricted myself to quoting the ancient sources, only mentioning modern works when essential. The reader should be aware that it is the current belief of professional ancient historians that military training in the form of the *ephēbeia* (the system of ephebic training) was only introduced in 335. It is also believed that the male, adult, Athenian citizenry also numbered 30,000 in the 4th century, not 20,000 as I propose here. I relish the opportunity to present the relevant evidence, both historical and archaeological, to the reader.

THE REFORMS OF CLEISTHENES

In 507, Cleisthenes introduced a new, democratic system in Athens. Previously, the political sympathies of the Athenians had largely been determined by the influence of important local families. The citizen body had been divided into four 'Ionic' tribes, presumably based on descent. Cleisthenes introduced ten new, totally artificial tribes (*phylai*) each consisting of three 'thirds' (*trittyes*) drawn one each from the city, the coast and inland. Each *tryttys* consisted of a variable number of villages or 'demes' (*dēmoi*). Cleisthenes named the demes after their principal localities, or some local hero (*AP* 21.5). About 140 demes have been identified at the time of writing. Each *tryttys* was made roughly equal numerically and they were matched together to make sure that the ten new tribes were, as much as possible, equal in number. According to Aristotle (*Politics* 3.1.10), Cleisthenes also enrolled into the tribes many foreigners and set free slaves resident in Attica. Decisions would be voted on by all male citizens who had reached their 20th year, meeting in an assembly (*ekklesia*). The business of the assembly would be prepared by a council of 500 (*boulē*), selected by lot, with 50 from each tribe. Each 50 selected from the tribe would hold the presidency (*prytany*) in turn, to be on hand to deal with emergencies.

A list of 100 Attic heroes was sent to Delphi for the Pythia, priestess of Apollo, to choose the ten names to be given to the ten new tribes. The Pythia selected the following names: I, Erechtheis; II, Aigeis; III, Pandionis; IV, Leontis; V, Akamantis; VI, Oineis; VII, Kekropis; VIII, Hippothontis; IX, Aiantis; and X, Antiochis. The order of the tribes is given as it was in the late 5th and early 4th centuries, but Raubitschek (1956) has offered different reconstructions of the order that might have been in force during the earlier 5th century.

The offices of the 'archon for war' (*polemarchos*) and general (*stratēgos*) had existed before the reform, but it was only eight years later in the archonship of Hermocreon (501/500) that the number of *stratēgoi* was brought up to ten, one being elected by each tribe and in command of the tribal regiment; the *polemarchos* remained in overall command (*AP* 22.2).

A hoplite is shown on this tondo (inside) of a broken *kylix* (drinking cup), decorated c.500 by an unidentified painter working in the wider circle of Nikosthenes. Wishing to minimize the area of his body exposed to archery, he crouches behind the cover of his shield. His Corinthian helmet is worn pulled down, his lower legs are defended by greaves and his spear is held at the ready. (Bryn Mawr College Special Collections, P.187)

This *kylix* in Cambridge (Fitzwilliam Museum GR 18.1937) was decorated by the 'Eucharides Painter' (Beazley 1963: 231,76), working *c.*500–470. It shows a line of hoplites, crouching and waiting 'in ambush' in a line of bushes. They are equipped only with spears, shields and helmets, their lower legs being protected by aprons hanging from the bottom of the shield, not greaves. Note the different devices decorating the shields. (Natalia Kozłowska)

THE PERSIAN WARS

At the battle of Marathon in 490, 'The right wing was commanded by the *polemarchos* Callimachus, for the law at that time demanded that the right wing should be led by the *polemarchos*. Under his leadership the tribes [*phylai*] followed in succession, according to the order of their numbers' (Herodotus, *Histories* 6.111), that is, the order of the tribes established by the Pythia. Pausanias notes that no more than 9,000 Athenians marched to Marathon 'including the old and slaves' (*Description of Greece* 10.20.2), while Herodotus tells us that the total number of Athenian males 'in the assembly' over the age of 20 was 30,000 (*Hist.* 5.97). Herodotus could either give that figure for the time he is discussing, *c.*500, or the time he was writing, later in the 5th century. Earlier on, Pausanias states (*Desc.* 7.15.7) that Miltiades and the Athenians set slaves free before the battle. Pausanias might be compressing events, since it seems to have been Cleisthenes who set free the slaves 12 years before the battle. The son of Miltiades was the influential politician Cimon, who did much to falsify the historical record to the benefit of his father. We can be sure, however, that each tribal regiment numbered 1,000.

A **THE BATTLE OF MARATHON**
This plate shows Athenian hoplites as they would have appeared around the time of Marathon, sheltering from the Persian cavalry in an olive grove sacred to Athena. The bronze greaves worn by all figures were of the 'anatomical' type, contoured to the muscles and held in place by the flexibility of bronze.
(1) Athenian hoplite
This individual wearing full armour is based on a figure shown on the Oxford Brygos Cup.
(2) Lightly clad hoplite
At Marathon the Athenians ran against the Persian forces (Herodotus, *Hist.* 6.122; Aristophanes, *Acharnians* 699), but the evidence of the Oxford Brygos Cup suggests they did not leave their armour behind. Nevertheless, we have chosen an alternative approach. The sparse evidence for family shield

emblems at Athens has been discussed elsewhere (Sekunda & McBride 1986: 10). In the early 5th century, most hoplites seem to have adopted shield devices appropriate to the god under whose protection they had placed themselves. In this case it is Dionysus, symbolized by a trefoil of ivy leaves, the ivy being sacred to that god.
(3) Athenian hoplite
This man has chosen to proclaim his wealth by choosing as his shield device the riding-box of a racing chariot, demonstrating that he is sufficiently wealthy to maintain a chariot team that has won a prize in an athletic competition. Shield devices could be chosen for a wide variety of reasons. He wears a helmet of the so-called 'Chalcidian' type, but in this case made up of iron plates used for the one-piece visor, plus nasal and neck-guard, while the skull is manufactured from iron scales.

Pinax (votive plaque) 'related to Euthymides' (Beazley 1963: 1598,5) in Athens (Acropolis Museum 1037). The name Megacles, who was ostracized in 486, has been scratched out, prompting suggestions that the figure of a silen, decorating this shield, was the shield device of the Megaclid branch of the Alcmaeonid family. The name Glauketes has been substituted. (Author's photograph)

The account of the command structure given by Herodotus (*Hist.* 6.109) is influenced by later practice, when command was rotated daily among the *stratēgoi*, and by political bias that led him to over-emphasize the role Miltiades played in the victory (Hignett 1952: 170–73). It seems the *stratēgoi* formed a consultative body, perhaps with a rotating presidency, but the *polemarchos* remained in overall command, as stated by the *Athēniaōn Politeia*. The account of the battle of Marathon in Herodotus fails to mention the presence of either Athenian cavalry or archers.

In 546 Cyrus the Great annexed Lydia, and the Greeks confronted the Achaemenid Empire for the first time. We have evidence that Greek hoplites took measures to minimize the effects of archery, which the Achaemenids disposed of in quantity, and some Greek armies were starting to acquire. One method to avoid injury from arrows was to maximize the area of the body that was protected by armour. We see hoplites start to wear protective armour plates on the upper arms and on the thigh: the lower leg already being protected by greaves. These new elements are shown on Attic vases, as well as testified to by actual examples. Some examples of ankle-guards have also been found (Everson 2004: 102–08).

Another method was to maximize mobility, and thereby minimize the time exposed to archery before closing with the enemy. Hoplites would 'strip' down to a minimum of armour, retaining only the hoplite shield, helmet and greaves, and run into battle against the enemy. The *hoplitodromos* ('armoured race') was introduced into the Olympic Games in 520 and the Pythian Games in 498. The first Greek athletic competition was a footrace run over one stade (185m) in the stadium (hence the name) at Olympia. The *hoplitodromos* was run over two stades, approximately equivalent to the range of an ancient bow.

Marathon to Plataea

The *Athēniaōn Politeia* tells us (22.5) that when Telesinos was archon (487/86) the Athenians started to appoint the archons, including the *polemarchos*, by lot, having previously elected them. Sortition, the method by which public officials were chosen by lot, was seen as a democratizing method of appointment, rather than election that could be influenced by bribery or favouritism. Nevertheless, it was unsafe to appoint a military commander by lot, and henceforward the *polemarchos* lost all military significance, other than performing sacrifices to Artemis Agrotera, goddess of the hunt, and Enyalios, god of war, and organizing the funeral games for the war dead (*AP* 58.1). Although elected to office in Anthesterion (February/March), the *stratēgoi*, like the archons and most other officials, took up their office on the first day of Hecatombaion.

The *stratēgos* was thereafter the sole significant office-holder to be elected directly, with the standing of his office enhanced at the expense of that of the older magistracies (Hignett 1952: 175). After the creation of the Athenian navy, *stratēgoi* could be appointed to a variety of command tasks and they started to acquire financial responsibilities as well as military. One *stratēgos* could be put in overall charge. Plutarch tells us (*Themistocles* 8.1) that at the battle of Salamis, Themistocles was the *stratēgos autokrator*, that is with overall power, but we do not know if he is being anachronistic. At first, each tribe elected one *stratēgos* from among its own members. From 441/40, however, we have evidence one tribe could supply more than one *stratēgos*. The *stratēgoi* were no longer responsible for the command of the tribal regiment, which was in future called a *taxis*, commanded by a *taxiarchos*. The *taxiarchoi* were instituted simultaneously with, or soon after, the reforms of 487/86. We do not know for sure on what basis the *taxiarchoi* held their rank. Isocrates implies (*Antidosis* 15.116) that the *stratēgos* appointed both the *taxiarchoi* and *lochogoi* beneath them, giving as his example the Athenian general Timotheus.

In the winter of 484/83 a fantastically rich vein of silver ore was discovered at Maroneia, in the district of Laurion, and Athens had a surplus of 100 talents from the workings. Some proposed this money should be distributed to the people, but Themistocles persuaded the people to lend to the wealthiest individuals of Athens one talent each, on condition that each of the 100 men took the responsibility to build one trireme (*AP* 22.7). In this way Themistocles had 100 triremes built. It was the first time the Athenians had a state fleet. Athens did not have the manpower to man both a fleet and field an army, however. The Athenians were absent from the battle of Thermopylae in 480 because they were fighting at Artemisium, but after Salamis, they participated with their land army in the Plataea campaign.

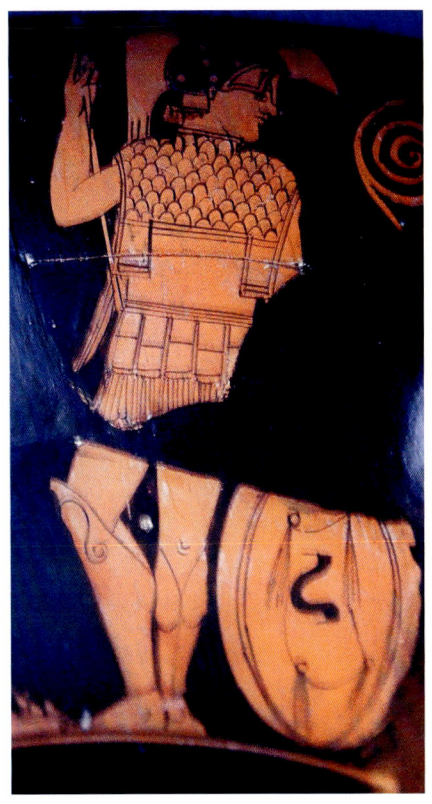

Detail from the Oxford Brygos Cup, painted shortly after the battle of Marathon and featuring participants in the battle. This warrior wears a composite cuirass made from panels of iron plates or scales covered by stiffened leather. The polished iron scales are left uncovered on the shoulder-guards. Plates of uncovered scale armour begin to be shown on Attic vase-paintings depicting the composite cuirass at the end of the 6th century, and areas decorated with lozenge-shaped patterns, which were probably inspired by the open scales, appear too. Helmets also start to be constructed of iron plates or scales. In this example the iron plates seem to be held in place by metal rivets allowed to protrude outside the cloth or leather covering of the skull helmet. He wears his cheek-guards up for comfort. (Author's photograph)

This amusing mug in Paris (Louvre Museum CA 2192), dating to 425–375, depicts a hoplite owl, the sacred bird of Athena. The owl's head is decorated with a transverse crest, which we have suggested was a badge of rank of the Athenian *lochagos*. (Marie-Lan Nguyen/Wikimedia/CC BY 2.5)

Formation of the Athenian archers

The 'Decree of Themistocles' (Fornara 1977: no. 55) is an inscription recording a decree moved by Themistocles to leave Athens for Salamis, and man 200 triremes and furnish four archers and ten naval hoplites (*epibatai*) between the ages of 20 and 30, the rest of the men to provide the oarsmen. So, it seems that in 480 Athens possessed a corps of 800 archers. This would not have been the first time that Athens had possessed a force of archers – indeed, we have plenty of pictorial evidence for Scythian archers in the employment of the Peisistratid tyranny – but it might be the first time that archers had been employed as far as the young Athenian democracy was concerned; employed, because archery requires constant practice to achieve a fair level of proficiency. In addition, such archers are likely to have been drawn from the poorer inhabitants of Athens, making it plausible for them to be paid (Van Wees 2013: 74). As Athenian archers were absent from the battle of Marathon, it would be logical to date their formation to 483 in line with Themistocles' plans to build a state fleet for the first time (Trundle 2010: 148).

The battle of Plataea

Herodotus tells us (*Hist.* 9.28) that at the battle of Plataea in 479, 8,000 Athenians occupied the left wing under the command of Aristeides, son of Lysimachus and one of the ten *stratēgoi* to have been elected for that year. Sophanetes of Deceleia proved himself the best of the Athenians on that day, his steadfastness being symbolized by the anchor he bore on his shield (Herodotus, *Hist.* 9.74). As well as the hoplite force, Athenian archers were present at the battle (9.22, 60). We do not know how the Athenian army was organized below the level of the tribal *taxis*, each numbering, presumably, 800 men. Before the battle the assembled Greek forces took a common oath, swearing that: 'I shall not fail the *taxilochos*, or the *enomotarch*, be he alive or dead, and I shall not retreat unless the *hegēmones* lead [the army] away, and I shall do whatever the *stratēgoi* command' (Fornara 1977: no. 60). These ranks can be regarded as referring to the allied army, and not an indication of the structure of the Athenian hoplite force.

The *lochos*

In the opening stages of the battle of Plataea the Megarians, hard pressed by the Persian cavalry under Masistius, had appealed for help. The Athenians volunteered, and sent 300 picked men commanded by Olympiodoros, son of Lampon, choosing the archers to aid them (Herodotus, *Hist.* 9.21–22). Plutarch describes Olympiodoros as 'the most zealous *lochagos*' of Aristeides' army (*Aristeides* 14.3), so the *lochos* seems to be a subdivision of the tribal *taxis*, but we cannot take its strength as 300. The troops under Olympiodoros were an ad hoc formation of volunteers, and 300 seems to have been the standard number for such forces (Barley 2015: 54). Thucydides also mentions (*History of the Peloponnesian War* 6.100.1) a picked *lochos* of 300 Athenian hoplites at Syracuse. Athenian *lochoi* are also mentioned by Plutarch (*Cimon* 17.5; *Pericles* 10.1).

It did not prove necessary to deploy the Athenian in full strength (*pandēmei* or *panstrateia*) on every campaign. For example, the army that fought at the battle of Spartolos in 429 numbered only 2,000 hoplites, but was divided into the normal ten tribal regiments. The Athenians were defeated and fell back on the two regiments guarding the baggage, which are named *phylai*

The crowning capital of an unusual three-sided monument, presumably funerary and from the modern-day town of Aigaleo (Egaleo), now in the Piraeus Museum (inv. 2575) and dated on stylistic grounds to the beginning of the 4th century. The symbolic significance of the two griffins is unknown; they usually guard treasure. Aigaleo, lying 4km west of Athens city centre, corresponds to the ancient deme Aigilia, named after a hero called Aegilos (Athenaeus, 16.652e), one of the 13 demes belonging to the tribe Antiochis. In the Roman army the transverse crest was a badge of rank for a centurion, and in the Athenian army it might have been the badge of rank for a *lochagos*. If so, this might have been the funerary monument, or a cenotaph, for an individual commanding a *lochos* raised in the deme Aigilia. (Author's photograph)

by Thucydides (*Hist*. 2.79.5). These tribal regiments would have numbered only 200 men each, but if the army was deployed in much more strength, it would have been convenient to divide the *taxis* into sub-units of manageable size. When the sailors were disembarked from their ships and sent to attack the Lacedaemonian hoplites on the island of Sphacteria in 424, they were organized in groups of roughly 200 men each (Thucydides, *Hist*. 4.32.3). This, then, was about the size of sub-unit that was thought convenient. The *lochos* could vary in size, but in general numbered 200 or 300 men (Xenophon, *Hellenica* 1.2.3). Xenophon (*Memorabilia* 3.4.1 cf. 4.1) lists *lochagoi* below *taxiarchoi* without any intervening rank.

The deme

We know from several passages, gathered by Crowley (2012), that *dēmotai*, men from the same deme, in times of war would fight together, just as in times of peace they would live together; they formed the 'primary group' that gave the Athenian hoplite the will to fight.

Three passages come from speeches of Lysias. Two of them describe the distribution of weapons within the deme. Lysias informs us (*Against Philon* 31.15–16) that Philon and many others contributed funds to arm his own fellow *dēmotai*. In another speech (*For Polystratos* 20.23), his fellow *dēmotai* testify to the number of times the father of Polystratos had served on campaign without avoiding his military service. A third passage (*For Mantitheos* 16.14) tells us that Mantitheos, when his *dēmotai* assembled to march to the relief of Haliartos in 395, gave 30 drachmas each to two of his fellow *dēmotai* as money for provisions (*ephodia*).

A speech of Isaeus (*On the Estate of Menekles* 2.42), dating to c.355, concerns the anonymous adopted son of Menekles, who says that he served in his tribe and in his deme on the campaigns that took place at this time. This anonymous individual also served as the *gymnasiarchos* in his father's deme and won credit as his adoptive father's son. So, this could be regarded as evidence that in demes with a *gymnasion*, the young men exercised together as well. Finally, one of Theophrastus' *Characters* (25.6), 'the coward', calls to his *dēmotai* and *phyletai* and tells them how he has been looking after a wounded comrade when he is absent from the battlefield.

The army would walk from their demes and assemble at the Lyceum, a *gymnasion* outside the city walls of Athens (Aristophanes, *Peace* 356; Xenophon, *Hell.* 1.1.33). Myronides, on being informed by the *lochagoi* that not all were present yet, said 'all are present that intend to fight' and led the army to victory, probably at Oinophyta in 457 (Plutarch, *Moralia* 185f–186a; cf. Diodorus Siculus, *Historical Library* 11.81.4–5). The *taxiarchoi* were responsible for noting people who had not turned up (Pollux, *Onomasticon* 8.115), and the punishment was loss of citizen rights and confiscation of property (Lysias, *Against Alcibiades* 14.9; Demosthenes, *Against Neaera* 59.27).

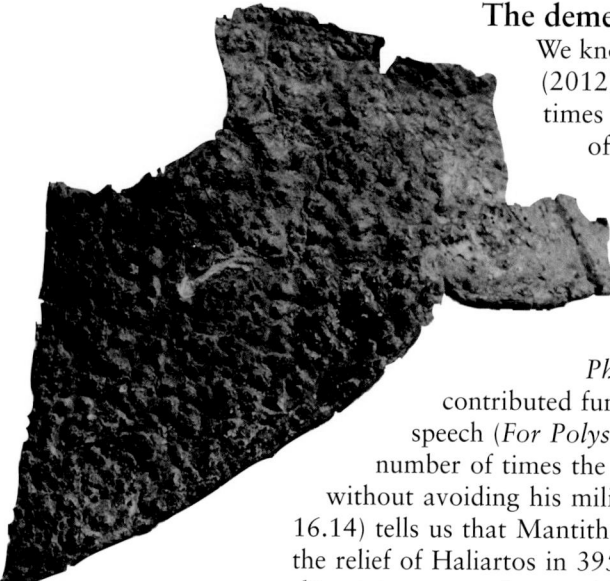

Fragment (above) of a cheek-piece from a Corinthian helmet seemingly taken as booty during Miltiades' expedition against Lemnos in 499 by the *dēmotai* of Rhamnous and dedicated in the temple of Nemesis, the principal sanctuary of the deme of Rhamnous. This illustration appeared in B. Petrakos, PAE 1984 A, 197–98, pl. 122 b, no. 92. The drawing (below) by K. Eliaki reveals how the cheek-piece is inscribed: 'The Rhamnousians dedicated [this, taken] on Lemnos, to Nemesis'. (Courtesy Archaeological Society at Athens)

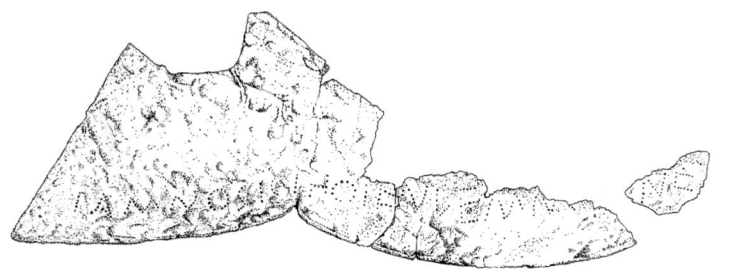

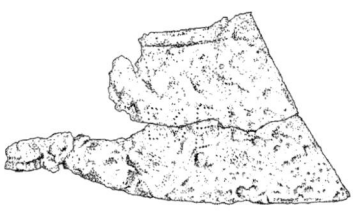

PAMMNOSIOIHOIENLEMMNOIANEOESANNEMESEI

This white-ground *lekythos* (jug) from Eretria, now in Athens (National Museum 1828), was decorated *c.*470–460 by the 'Providence Painter' (Beazley 1963: 642,113). It shows a youth holding two spears, dressed in a black *chlamys* and a *petasos* and inscribed 'Glaucon is beautiful'. The colour black was associated with death, and the black cloak is symbolic of the exclusion of the *ephēbos* from normal social life. It could possibly be the first depiction of an Athenian *ephēbos*. (Author's photograph)

LIABILITY FOR MILITARY SERVICE

Liability for military service, and ephebic service, seems to have been practically universal. Lysias informs us (*On the Refusal of a Pension* 24.13) that in Athens an invalid was entitled to draw a pension of one obol a day. The detailed regulations changed later for the *Athēniaōn Politeia* inform us (49.4) that the law prescribed that men who possessed less than three mina (400 drachmas) and men who were so maimed in their bodies that they cannot do any work, were to be scrutinized by the *boulē* and given two obols a day. The register of invalids is also mentioned by Aeschines (*Against Timarchus* 1.103).

Certain categories of citizens were exempt from mobilization. As well as the invalids, these included those currently serving on the *boulē*. It seems, however, that the average age for service on the *boulē* was at least 40, so this did not amount to many. Those currently engaged in litigation were also exempt from military service. Andocides (*Against Alcibiades* 4.22) refers scornfully to the young men who were in court while the old men were out fighting. Isaeus (*For Callius* 5.46) claims that Dikaiogenes, though an Athenian citizen, had not served once during the present war, by which he seems to mean the Corinthian War (395–387).

Registration in the deme

When a male child had completed his 17th year, his name was entered on the list of citizens (*lexiarchicon grammateion*) for the deme in which his father was registered. Athenian personal names were made up of three elements: the person's name, the person's father's name (patronymic) and the name of the deme in which the person was registered (demotic). This listing of names took place, presumably, at the beginning of the Athenian year in Hecatombaion. A fragment of Antidotus from his play entitled *Protochoros* ('First Dancer') and preserved in Athenaeus (*Deipnosophists* 6.240c) has a young man say: 'before I was enrolled in my deme and received my ephebe's cloak'. Antidotus was an Athenian comic poet of whom we know next to nothing, except that one of his plays was ascribed to him, but also to Alexis, whom we know to have been active *c.*340–330. Consequently, we cannot be sure if Antidotus was writing before or after the reform of the *ephēbeia* in 335.

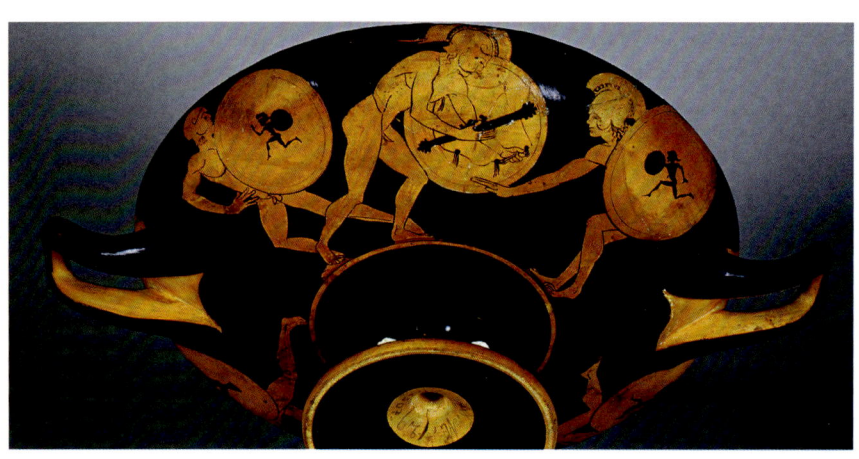

On this Attic *kylix*, painted *c.*495–480 by the 'Antiphon Painter' (Beazley 1963: 341,77), one young man shows another the best start position for the *hoplitodromos*. The set of shields they are using are not decorated with any religious symbol, but a symbol referring to athleticism, a running man. Perhaps they were owned by a private training establishment or a deme *gymnasion*. (Antikensammlung, Staatlicher Museen zu Berlin inv. F 2307, Ingrid Geske)

On the other side of the same drinking cup is shown a runner with a shield decorated with the same device, a running man, competing against runners with different shield devices. Again, these have no perceptible religious significance, so they perhaps were owned by rival *gymnasia*. (Antikensammlung, Staatlicher Museen zu Berlin inv. F 2307, Ingrid Geske)

Two months later, in the month of Boedromion (September/October), the young men went to the Temple of Aglauros and took the 'ephebic oath', stating that among other things, they would not disgrace their arms, would not desert their comrades, and would obey their commanders. According to Plutarch (*Alcib.* 15.4), in the aftermath of the Battle of Mantineia in 418 Alcibiades counselled the Athenians to maintain in deed the oath regularly taken by the *ephēboi* in the Temple of Aglauros. In his speech *On the Embassy* (19.303), delivered in 343, Demosthenes refers to his rival Aeschines reading out the oath taken by the *ephēboi* in the Temple of Aglauros. In his speech *Against Leocrates* (76), delivered in 330, Lycurgus refers to the oath sworn by all citizens, 'as they are enrolled in the *lexiarchicon grammateion*', then proceeds to give the oath. So, the point at which the oath was taken might have changed with the reform. According to Diodorus Siculus (*Hist.* 11.3), the same oath was first taken for the first time by all the Greek forces at the Isthmus on the eve of the Plataea campaign, giving a slightly different version of the oath.

The tondo of the same cup shows a single athlete, presumable the winner of the *hoplitodromos*, with his shield decorated with the device of a running man. (Antikensammlung, Staatlicher Museen zu Berlin inv. F 2307, Ingrid Geske)

At some point in his induction into the *ephēbeia*, the Athenian *ephēbos* would be given a cloak, presumably on his taking the oath. Athenian *ephēboi* wore a black *chlamys* until AD 165/66, when Herodes Atticus paid for their replacement with white ones, 'for before that time they had worn black cloaks whenever they sat in a group at public meetings, or marched in festal processions, in token of the public mourning of the Athenians for the herald Copreus, whom they themselves had slain when he was trying to drag the sons of Heracles from the altar' (Philostratus, *Lives of the Sophists* 2.1.4). This action of Herodes Atticus is also attested in an inscription (*IG* ii² 2090, 5–10). According to a fragment of Philemon preserved in Pollux (*On.* 10.164), *ephēboi* also wore a *petasos* hat as well as their *chlamys*. Philemon was a comic poet working in Athens from *c.*330 onwards, where he was awarded Athenian citizenship.

The individual spent the next two years as an *ephēbos*, a term given to young men 'arrived at their prime' [*hēbē*], during which he was liable for military service within the borders of Attica. On entering his 20th year he became liable for military service outside the borders of Attica, an obligation that lasted until his 50th year. He remained liable for military service within the borders of Attica until his 60th year.

According to the *Athēniaōn Politeia* (53.4), all the 42 year-classes were named after different heroes. When a man reached his 60th year he was de-registered, and a new list was opened for those who were in their 18th year under the same hero name. This was presumably to eliminate any confusion if archons of the same name were appointed for different years. The names of the year-class 'used to be listed on white-washed tablets, together with the name of the archon in whose year they were enrolled' (*AP* 53.4). So, the *dēmarchos*, responsible for the administration of the deme, was responsible for maintaining all 42 such lists kept by archon year.

Young cavalryman fighting an Amazon shown on a white-ground *lekythos* in Boston (MFA 01.8147 Henry Lillie Pierce Fund), bought in Athens and decorated *c.*440. (© Boston MFA)

B

TRAINING
(1) Athlete training for the *hoplitodromos*
Runners in the *hoplitodromos* were equipped with a shield, helmet and greaves, but no cuirass. The wearing of greaves was discontinued after *c.*450. It is sometimes difficult to decide if a *hoplitodromos* or a military event is being shown on a given Athenian vase. The *hoplitodromos*, as it was an athletic event, was run naked, whereas, if the context is military, the hoplite generally wears an *ephaptis* 'wrap-around' cloak about his loins. If spears are being carried, it is likely to be a military scene, it being too dangerous to carry them in the *hoplitodromos*.

The *hoplitodromos* was run with a set of competition shields specially designed to be of equal, and perhaps reduced, weight. These were stored in temples or arsenals, where they can be described by the diminutive term *aspidiskoi* in the inventories that were periodically carried out and recorded in inscriptions. If used in games held to honour a particular god, all the set of shields would be decorated with symbols associated with the god: for example, a swastika sun-symbol, which was associated with Apollo; or perhaps the initials of the god, 'ΑΘΗ' for Athena for example. In the example illustrated here, the young athlete carries a shield decorated with the figure of an athlete running in the *hoplitodromos*. *Ephēboi* and older young men would participate in the *hoplitodromos*.

(2) Athenian *ephēbos*
This figure is based on an Attic *lekythos* dating to 470–460 and showing a young man wearing a black *chlamys* and *petasos*, carrying a pair of hunting spears. Hunting was a favourite pursuit of young men.

(3) Ephebic cavalryman (?)
I have suggested before (Sekunda & McBride 1986: 19), based on a white-ground *lekythos* dating to *c.*415 and showing a young horseman dressed in a black cloak, that it is conceivable that ephebic training was extended to young cavalrymen at that time. Subsequent research has shown that the depiction of young horsemen wearing black cloaks goes back farther than that. This figure is based on another white-ground *lekythos* in Boston dating to *c.*440: a couple of years after the suggested date for the cavalry reform attributed to Pericles.

One of the skills demanded of the Athenian *hippeis* was javelin-throwing from horseback, which is attested in 5th-century vases. In fact, Sir John Beazley, running out of fresh names, came up with the designation 'Hippakontist Painter' (Beazley 1963: 769–770) for a minor artisan active in the second quarter of the 5th century with a predilection for painting such scenes on his produce. Training in this skill at this early date was poorly organized, if at all. Plato records (*Meno* 93d) that Themistocles personally instructed his son Cleophantus in horse-riding and in throwing a javelin from horseback, though this could date to Themistocles' period of exile.

The liability for service of the *ephēboi* and men in the 50th to 59th year-groups within the borders of Attica is demonstrated by events of 458/57 (Thucydides, *Hist*. 1.105.4–106.2). The Corinthians, thinking that the Athenians would be forced to break off their siege of Aegina, against which they had deployed all their forces, occupied the heights of Geraneia and descended on Megara, which was allied with Athens. But the Athenians called out 'such forces as were left in the city, consisting of their oldest and youngest men' and dispatched this force into the Megarid under the famous general Myronides. By 'oldest', Thucydides has in mind those men aged between their 50th and 59th year, and by 'youngest' those in their 18th or 19th year. One indecisive battle was fought, then a second one at Kimolia 12 days later. The Corinthian hoplites were thrown back, and, in their confusion, a considerable proportion of them lost their way and rushed into some farmland enclosed by a great ditch. It was a dead end. The Athenian hoplites barred the entrance while the *psiloi* stoned to death the Corinthian hoplites trapped inside.

The word *psilos* is usually applied to a lightly armed combatant, but in this context, it is more likely that it can be taken to mean non-combatant 'attendants'. When Herodotus (*Hist*. 9.30) calculates the total manpower fielded by the Greeks at Plataea, he assumes that each hoplite was accompanied by a *psilos*. In Athens, a slave society, it was normal for an individual citizen of sufficient wealth to serve as a hoplite and to have his own personal slave. In time of war, the slave would carry the hoplite's bedding and rations for him. Usually referred to as *skeuophoroi*, or 'baggage carriers' in our texts, the slaves would participate in the battle only if an unusual opportunity arose. Their essential role was recognized by the Athenian state. Thucydides reports (*Hist*. 3.17.3) that the hoplites at the siege of Potidaea in 432 received a campaign allowance of two drachmas a day: one drachma for themselves, and one drachma for their attendants.

The ephebic torch-races

We have evidence for three ephebic torch-races before the reform of the *ephēbeia* in 335, connected with the festivals of Prometheus, Hephaistos and Pan, the last of which took place during the Panathenaic festival. The torch-race for the Hephaisteia was a relay race, but the two others were individual.

Some information concerning the Panathenaic torch-race is contained in Aristophanes' *Frogs*, performed in 405. It seems that the race started in the Kerameikos (131), and, indeed, the scholia to this passage and to v.1087 indicate that all three torch-races started there. Later on, Aristophanes informs us that 'from lack of athletic training nobody is able any longer now to carry the torch' (vv.1087–88). He continues to describe how a laggard in the race, who has run into difficulties, is physically tormented by the people living in the Kerameikos. This passage makes little sense unless these torch-races were a compulsory part of ephebic training. It is hard to see why anyone in poor physical condition would take part in the race unless it was compulsory. Plato informs us (*Crito* 50d) that the laws of the state require fathers to educate their sons in music and physical exercise (*gymnastikē*). It is probable that Plato has in mind the choral competitions and the ephebic torch-races.

A single inscription (*IG* ii² 1250) has been preserved, recording a victory of the tribe Aiantis in the torch-race of the Hephaisteia in some unknown year around the 350s or 340s, and the decision of the tribe to honour the *gymnasiarchos* Epis(tratos?), son of Trempon the Rhamnousian (Sekunda 1990).

Many wealthy Athenian young men copied Thessalian dress in the 5th century, as is shown on many red-figure vases, rarely in polychrome. A young man, standing beside his own tomb, carrying two spears used in hunting, rather than fighting, is shown in this white-ground *lekythos* in Athens (National Museum inv. A.1935) decorated by the 'Bosanquet Painter' (Beazley 1963: 1227,1). It was found in Eretria and dates to *c*.450–440. (Wojciech Brillowski)

The *gymnasiarchia* for each of the three competitions, particularly the Prometheia, could prove to be an expensive undertaking and it was taken up on an annual basis by only the wealthier members of the tribe. In a speech written by Lysias (*Defence Against a Charge of Taking Bribes* 21.3) and delivered in 403/02 by an unknown plaintiff, he says he served as *gymnasiarchos* for the Prometheia and won after spending more than 12 minae (one mina equalled 100 drachmas). In a speech of Isaeus (*On the Estate of Apollodorus* 7.36), composed not long after 357/56 for one Thrasyllus, the plaintiff states that that he has acted as *gymnasiarchos* in the Prometheia that year 'with a liberality which all my fellow tribesmen acknowledge'.

Property-owning groups

A puzzling passage in Pollux (*On.* 8.130) dealing with four property-owning classes is translated and discussed by Van Wees, who concludes that

The name vase of the 'Dokimasia Painter' (Beazley 1963: 412,1), this *kylix* in Berlin (Antikensammlung, Berlin, Schloss Charlottenburg, F2296), found in Orvieto, Italy, shows the *dokimasia* of the cavalry horses of the *hippeis* by the *boulē*, which was first depicted on vases dating from *c*.510 (Bugh 1988: 14–20), and so pre-dates Pericles. The scribe sitting to the right notes the result of the inspection. (Natalia Kozłowska)

it must reflect some reform of the taxation system under Cleisthenes (Van Wees 2013: 93). The *pentakosiomedimnoi*, producing 500 dry and liquid measures, paid one talent into the public treasury; the *hippeis* produced 300

The tondo of the same vase depicts a Scythian horse-archer testing an arrow for straightness. We can perhaps connect this with the 'purchase' of 300 Scythian archers (Trundle 2010: 149) at the same time as the *hippeis* was expanded to 300 in number. (Natalia Kozłowska)

measures and paid half a talent; the *zeugitai* produced 200 measures and paid 10 minae; and the *thetes* were exempt from payment. The treasurers of Athena were chosen only from the *pentakosiomedimnoi*, the archons only from the members of the first two classes (Hignett 1952: 142). The *thetes* held no office at all. The lower threshold of 200 measures set for the *zeugitai*, 'owners of a yoke of ploughing oxen', who were supposed to supply the hoplites to the army was not much lower than the 300 measures set for the *hippeis*, and, according to the calculations of Van Wees (2013: 87), this equates to the yield from a plot of 40 acres, sufficient to sustain 15 people. The *hippeis*, the 'knights', were supposed to supply the cavalry.

EARLY ATHENIAN CAVALRY

Our knowledge of early Athenian cavalry is entirely dependent on our understanding of an enigmatic Athenian institution known as the *naukraria*. In the Archaic period the citizens of the Greek city states principally had to find funding for only two major state expenses: namely temple-building and maintaining military forces. As far as temples are concerned, we have information on several ambitious building programmes from the earlier period of the Peisistratid tyranny. One of them, the Olympieion, was not completed until the reign of the Roman Emperor Hadrian (r. AD 117–38). No expense was required for the hoplites: citizens who fell at or above the wealth bracket for hoplite service were simply required to equip themselves as hoplites and turn up. It was different for cavalry. If an, admittedly wealthy, individual was to be induced to supply his horse for military use, who was to pay for its fodder in peacetime, and who would compensate

Parthenon West frieze, Slab IV, showing figures W7 and W8. On figure W8 (left), the upper seam of the tunic hanging down from the shoulder and the boots can barely be seen. Originally, the frieze would have been painted and these details would have been more evident. (Universal History Archive/Universal Images Group via Getty Images)

Parthenon, West frieze, Slab IX, showing figures W16 and W17. The broad-rimmed Thessalian hat worn by W17 was made of felt. It was large and of a very distinctive shape, because the brim was folded down in two places on either side, billowing out at the ear, to allow it to be tied in place by a cord tied under the neck, or at the occiput. Traces of green paint were found on the cloak. (Universal History Archive/ Universal Images Group via Getty Images)

him if it were lost or crippled on campaign? The embryonic finances of the early Athenian state had to grapple with these two problems. On *naukraria*, Pollux runs thus:

> Demarchs: those who are in charge of each deme. For a time they were called *naukraroi*, when the demes too [were called] *naukrariai*. A *naukraria* was, for a time, the twelfth part of a tribe, and there were twelve *naukraroi*, four to each *trittys*. These men handled the revenues of the demes and their expenditures. Each *naukraria* supplied two horsemen and one ship, from which it perhaps acquired its name. (*On.* 8.108; Fornara 1977: no. 22B)

The word *naukraria* can either be derived from the word *naus* ('ship') or *naos* ('temple'), as pointed out by Billigmeier and Dusing (1981). As we have seen, before 483 the Athenian state did not own a single ship. Warships were provided by wealthy private individuals in a manner resembling the corsairs of the early modern period. Indeed, Themistocles, when the first Athenian state fleet was built, lent the money out to wealthy individuals to build a ship each. Athens had no experience in funding naval production in any other way. It might have been inconceivable to Pollux, writing in the 2nd century AD, that Athens, even in the 6th century BC, did not have a state fleet, but it did not. Even Pollux admits to doubts as to the derivation of the name.

Most modern authorities agree that the *naukraroi* appear to have been wealthy individuals organized into taxation groups called *naukrariai* arranged on a territorial bases rather than units of local government. According to

Bust of Pericles, in all probability the author of the reforms in the Athenian cavalry, in the Vatican Museum (inv. 269). According to Plutarch, 'his head was rather long and out of due proportion, for this reason the images of him, almost all of them, wear helmets, because the artists, as it would seem, were not willing to reproach him with deformity' (*Pericles* 3.2). The Corinthian helmet was already falling out of favour in the middle of the 5th century. Thanks to Pericles' deformity, hidden by the Corinthian helmet pushed back on the crown of the head, the popularity of that type of helmet for later portraits of Athenian *stratēgoi* was established. This Roman copy was found in a villa near Tivoli, along with a multitude of other portraits. (Bartosz Buszman)

Cleidemus, in a fragment preserved in Photius' *Lexicon* (Fornara 1977: no. 22A), Cleisthenes increased the number of *naukrariai* to 50. If we are to take Pollux at face value, then the Athenian cavalry may have numbered 100 immediately after the reforms of Cleisthenes, though we have no evidence to support this (Bugh 1988: 4–6; Van Wees 2013: 74).

The strength of the cavalry was later expanded to 300. Both Aeschines (*On the Embassy* 2.173) and Andocides (*On the Peace with Sparta* 3.5) make this coterminous with the building of the 'Long Walls' connecting Athens with Piraeus, which was carried out in 457. Both sources also mention the 'purchase' of 300 Scythian archers at the same time. A statue base found before the Propylaea on the Acropolis (*IG* i² 400) bears the inscription:

> The horsemen [dedicated this monument] from
> the spoils of war; the *hipparchoi* were
> Lakedaimonios, Xenophon, and Pronapes.
> Lykios, son of Myron, from Eleutherae made it.

The number of *hipparchoi* was evidently three, which was presumably dictated by the way the 300-strong cavalry force was organized internally. This inscription has been dated to 457, the year of the battle of Oinophyta. The Lakedaimonios honoured in this inscription is the son of Cimon, and Bugh (1988: 47) has suggested that Cimon might have been behind the expansion in the number of the cavalry. We know that Cimon wrote a work entitled *Hipposkopikon* ('Horse Inspection'; *Suda* K 1621), and he could have written it for use during the *dokimasia*, the annual inspection of horse and rider before the *boulē*, for the benefit of his son Lakedaimonios. The *dokimasia* is recorded on Athenian vases dating back to *c.*510, so it could date back to the reforms of Cleisthenes or even earlier (Bugh 1988: 14–20).

5TH-CENTURY ATHENIAN CAVALRY

The plate recreates the images of three horsemen from the West frieze of the Parthenon. The frieze was sculpted between *c.*443 and *c.*437 and probably depicts the procession of the Greater Panathenaic festival from the Leokoreion by the Dipylon Gate up to the Parthenon. The 'Greater' Panathenaic festival, during which weapons would not be carried, was celebrated every four years, the 'Lesser' Panathenaia annually. Horsemen take up nearly half the length of the frieze. Despite repeated attempts to detect 'uniformity' in the dress worn by the horsemen, Stevenson (2003) is probably correct in stating that at this time, dress depended entirely on the personal choice of the cavalryman.

(1) Athenian cuirassed cavalryman

This depiction is based on figure W7. On the sculpture, the folds in the 'overfall' of the tunic tied at the waist can be seen beneath the cuirass. He wears a 'muscle-cuirass' without shoulder-guards, so as not to impede javelin-throwing.

(2) Cavalryman wearing Thracian dress

This depiction is based on figure W8. All figures of horsemen shown on the Parthenon frieze are beardless youths except for two, W8 and W15, who along with S2–S7 wear Thracian dress. Thracians wore fox-skins on their heads, multi-coloured, patterned cloaks and boots of doeskin reaching up to the knee (Herodotus, *Hist.* 7.75). This figure wears a normal Greek tunic, but a Thracian hat, cloak and boots. It is uncertain whether the neck-flap to the hat was made of fox-skin or of multi-coloured Thracian textile, and it could have ended in a right angle, or had the shape of a 'beaver's tail'. Robertson and Frantz (1975: ad pl. VIII 15) suggest that these bearded figures, on account of their senior age are *hipparchoi*, which seems reasonable, but the fact that they both wear Thracian dress may be coincidental. In the Archaic period, influential Athenian families had estates or castles in the coastal regions of Thrace: perhaps these Thracian contacts were maintained.

(3) Cavalryman in Thessalian dress

Based on W17 from Slab IX, this rider wears a Thessalian hat and cloak. Many prominent Athenian aristocratic families maintained close relationships with their Thessalian counterparts and imitated their dress. The Thessalian type of cloak, usually with a different-coloured border at either side, was wrapped around the left shoulder and pinned with a fibula above the right shoulder. It hung round the body in a very distinctive way, hanging in a V-shape at the front and back and open on the right-hand side.

This helmet (Ephorate of Antiquities of the City of Athens Δ 2377) was found in a cist grave in Odos Madytou, together with an iron sword and an alabastron during rescue excavations. This photograph taken from the original excavation report (Alexandri 1973: pl. 52a) demonstrates that, unlike the *petasos* hat, the helmet was worn with the brim level to the skull, not perched at a rakish angle, as the Athenian *hippeis* preferred. The excavator (Alexandri 1973) identified it as an early version of the 'Boeotian' helmet, but it lacks the double indentation of the brim, which was a hallmark of the Boeotian type. I termed this helmet the '*petasos*-helmet' from its general resemblance in shape to the *petasos* hat (Sekunda & McBride 1986: 19). (Courtesy Archaeological Society at Athens)

The cavalry reform of Pericles

Albert Martin (1887: 134) suggested that it was during the archonship of Diphilos in 442/41 that the number of Athenian cavalry expanded to 1,000, probably by a law moved by Pericles. Each of the ten Athenian tribes supplied a tribe (*phylē*) of 100 commanded by a *phylarchos*. The ten *phylai* of horse were under the command of two *hipparchoi* who would each command a wing of five *phylai* in battle. All these officers were elected annually.

The cavalry, like the hoplites, were not paid a regular wage, but unlike the hoplites they were given a daily fodder allowance (*sitos*) of one drachma in times of peace or war alike. The expansion of the cavalry was facilitated by the introduction of the *katastasis* or 'establishment grant', which the Athenian cavalryman received upon joining the corps. This guaranteed the replacement cost of any mount lost on service, but was repayable on leaving the corps. To avoid fraudulent claiming of allowances, each cavalryman who had been paid the *katastasis* was required to present a serviceable horse at a *dokimasia* of the cavalry before the *boulē* of Athens, following the election of the officers. Each rider and horse would be carefully inspected for fitness for service. Horses that failed to pass the *dokimasia* were branded on the jaw with the sign of a wheel, to prevent them being slipped through the *dokimasia* on a future occasion (*AP* 49.1).

The Greeks (other than Xenophon) did not differentiate from one type of bronze helmet in the shape of a felt hat to the next. To them they were all 'piloi' (the word for felt). In the *Lysistrata* (562), produced in 411, Aristophanes pokes fun at the *phylarchos* who eats *alphita* (pearl-barley gruel) out of his 'pilos', which obviously was not a felt hat. Paradoxically, this helmet from Odos Madytou has small holes along the brim, suggesting it was covered with felt, reminiscent of the 'steel hat' of the early modern period. (Wojciech Brillowski)

This Attic white-ground *lekythos* from Eretria and now in Athens (National Museum 1818), painted by the 'Achilles Painter' (Beazley 1963: 998, 161), dates from *c.*440. Around the middle of the 5th century, it became fashionable to paint an 'apotropaic' eye on the shield, to look out for incoming missiles; this one is located on a circular 'medallion', also very popular at the time. (DeAgostini/Getty Images)

This partially preserved relief stored in Eleusis Archaeological Museum (inv. 5101) is inscribed: '[Pythodoro]s, son of Epizelos, having served as *hipparchos* [dedicated this to the gods]' (*IG* i² 816). It shows a clash between invading Peloponnesian infantry and Athenian cavalry sometime during the 420s (Bugh 1988: 91–93). This relief encapsulates the role of the Athenian cavalry, envisaged for it by Pericles (Spence 1990), in doing much to limit the damage done to the Attic countryside by preventing enemy infantry spread out to devastate the countryside. Both registers show Peloponnesian hoplites – one, appropriately, wearing a *pilos* helmet – being attacked by Athenian horse from the right. The *hipparchos* is shown in the upper register, wearing a muscle-cuirass and, probably, a helmet rather than a hat. (Author's photograph)

These payments were made from the regular Athenian state income, in times of peace as well as war, and represented a considerable imposition on the state budget. In practice, epigraphic evidence (*IG* i³ 375) shows that in the year 410/09, for example, during the Peloponnesian War (431–404), the Athenians fielded barely half that number of cavalry (Spence 1987). The Athenians, under the leadership of Pericles, now possessed a cavalry arm equal to that of the principal ally of the Lacedaemonians, Boeotia, and inferior only to that of Thessaly. This meant that the Athenians could now challenge the Lacedaemonians for the leadership of the Greek world.

A unit of 200 horse-archers was also raised, presumably on a tribal basis: Alcibiades the Younger, son of Alcibiades, was expelled from the horse-archers of his *phylē* by his *phylarchos* (Lysias, *Against Alcibiades* 15.5). The horse-archers were deployed in front of the cavalry and rode ahead of the *hipparchoi* (Xenophon, *Mem.* 3.3.1). A single *hippo[toxatēs]* is attested in a list of fallen Athenian citizens belonging to an unknown tribe from, reputedly, the first half of the 5th century (*IG* i³ 1192, 158–59).

Tombstone of Sosias and Kephisdōros (Antikensammlung, Staatlicher Museen zu Berlin Sk. 1708), dating to *c*.410. The man standing on the left wearing the unbelted long tunic is a priest. The central figure, presumably Sosias, again grips his spear-butt in his left hand, and at the same time with his left index finger he holds the rope fore-handle (*antilabē*) of the hoplite shield, which is not shown on the relief, but would have been painted on the stone afterwards, like the continuation of the spear-shaft. The figure standing to the right is presumably Kephisdōros. (Dorota Sakowicz)

THE PELOPONNESIAN WAR

Thucydides (*Hist.* 2.13.6–8) gives the strength of the Athenian army on the outbreak of the Peloponnesian War as follows: 13,000 citizen hoplites of military age; 16,000 *ephēboi*, old men and metics (*metoikoi* were foreign citizens permanently resident in Athens), all of which categories could, under normal circumstances, only be mobilized for the defence of Attica; 1,200 cavalry, including the 200 horse-archers; 1,600 foot-archers; and 300 seaworthy triremes. The triremes would have required over 50,000 oarsmen if fully manned. Consequently, the Athenians were dependent on foreigners to crew their navy, which was practicable if the resources of empire were sufficient to pay them (Thucydides, *Hist.* 1.143.1), but in straitened circumstances the Athenians had to row their own ships.

The *taxiarchos*

Aristophanes makes numerous references to the badges of rank of the *taxiarchos*: the three crests that adorn his helmet, and his crimson cloak. Aristophanes' *Peace* was produced at the City Dionysia in spring 421. The chorus in line 395 refers to being sickened by Peisander's crests: Peisander

This grave stele of Chairedēmos and Lykeias, found in Salamis and now in the Piraeus Museum (inv. 385; *IG*² ii 13030) can be dated on stylistic grounds to *c*.420–410. Chairedēmos, shown on the left, holds his bronze spear-butt in his left hand, a habit which is increasingly found around these times. Maybe he holds the fore-handle with his little finger. He has chosen to expose his body to view, despite the cloak draped over his shoulders. Lykeias also holds his spear by the butt, but in the right hand, and he is fully clothed. Paradoxically, both figures appear to be shod. (George E. Koronaios/ Wikimedia/CC BY-SA 4.0)

may well have been a *taxiarchos* in 422/21. In Aristophanes' *Acharnians*, produced for the Lenaea in 425, several remarks are made with reference to Lamachus, who was not a *stratēgos* at this time, but may have been a *taxiarchos*. Repeated references or allusions are made to crests (567, 575, 967) or triple crests (965, 1109). At line 1103, Lamachus asks for the two plumes from his helmet to be brought to him, and at 1105 he remarks that the ostrich plume is beautiful and white. It is unlikely that the *taxiarchos* wore a simple *pilos* helmet, but rather a helmet capable of bearing a central horsehair crest, probably white in colour, with two plumes of white ostrich feathers worn on both sides. We have some evidence for badges of rank being borne on the Corinthian helmet, which was made popular by Pericles.

In *Acharnians* too, numerous references are made to the *gorgoneion* shield device on Lamachus' shield (574, 964, 1095, 1124, 1131, 1181). In *Peace* at line 561, Aristophanes has Trygaeus say 'praise to the goddess who has got rid of those crests and gorgons'. In the *Lysistrata*, produced in 411, Aristophanes says at line 560, that a man with a shield with a gorgon on it buying small fish in the market is a ridiculous spectacle. The implication of this statement is that the *gorgoneion* was not a shield device confined to *taxiarchoi*, but could be borne by all Athenians of a warlike nature. In *Electra* at line 1257, and likewise in *Ion* at line 210, Euripides refers to the shield of Athena bearing a gorgon as its shield device. Paradoxically, depictions of the *gorgoneion* shield device are rather rare in Athenian vase-paintings.

D ATHENIAN HOPLITES DURING THE 5TH CENTURY

All these figures carry hoplite spears about 2.4m in length, each with a small leaf-shaped iron spearhead and cylindrical bronze spear-butt. By this time, greaves have been abandoned in the search for mobility. All the hoplites are shown barefoot, as they are in all forms of Greek art. The normal Athenian hoplite was a farmer who worked barefoot in the fields, took his physical exercise barefoot, even naked, and saw no need to don footwear when called upon to perform military service. Boots were worn for specific purposes, such as for hunting, in which the hunter was likely to have to run through prickly undergrowth.

Footwear would not be worn by infantry unless it was extremely cold. When texts mention soldiers barefoot, they generally do so in a context in which all the troops have been overtaken by winter while dressed in their summer clothing. Xenophon tells us (*Hell.* 2.1.1) that after the disastrous naval battle of Arginusae in 406, the Athenian troops that were left on Chios under the command of Eteonicus, as long as the summer lasted, existed upon the produce of the season and by working for hire up and down the island. When winter came on, however, and they were without food, poorly clothed and unshod, they got together and agreed to make an attack upon Chios. The same thing happened to the Athenian forces when they were surprised by the unusually severe winter of 430/29 in Chalcidice. Plato tells us that 'in those parts the winters are awful', and while the other Athenians 'wrapped ourselves up with prodigious care, and after putting on our shoes we muffled up our feet with felt and little fleece', Socrates 'walked out in that weather, clad in just such a cloak [*himation*] as he was always wont to wear, and he made his way more easily over the ice unshod than the rest of us did in our shoes' (*Symp.* 220a–c). Socrates never wore shoes (Xenophon, *Mem.* 1.6.2).

In the decades around the end of the 5th century and the beginning of the 4th century, nakedness became very frequent in depictions of Athenian warriors, whether in sculpture or in the fast-disappearing painted vases. This might not be so fantastic as it seems at first. Warriors exercised naked, and warfare was an activity from which women were largely excluded. A recent work (Murray 2022) explores the universality of nudity in Greek art and culture.

We have no evidence of any uniformity in dress in the Athenian army at this period. Some Athenians were killed at the battle of Delium in 424. The Thespian contingent stood their ground while the other Boeotians had fled. The Athenians enveloped them, and 'getting into confusion owing to their surrounding the enemy killed one another' (Thucydides, *Hist.* 4.96.3).

(1) Hoplite, c.440
From the middle of the 5th century onwards, the cuirass and greaves were worn less and less, as full-scale pitched battles became more infrequent. The Corinthian helmet dominated the scene for most of the 5th century, but then lost its popularity.

(2) Hoplite, c.410
This figure is based on the central figure depicted on the tombstone of Sosias and Kephisdōros. During the Peloponnesian War, the Athenian forces adopted the *pilos* helmet, which practically displaced the Corinthian and all other forms of helmet. This was because the *pilos* helmet offered advantages in terms of visibility and light weight that made it suitable for campaigns rather than pitched battles. Another factor could be military 'fashion' – the Lacedaemonian army, which was the first to adopt the *pilos* helmet, was the pre-eminent military force in the Greek world at the time.

(3) Taxiarchos
This figure represents an attempt to reconstruct the appearance of a *taxiarchos* based on passages in Aristophanes.

A Corinthian helmet fitted with an arrangement of plumes exactly the same as that described by Aristophanes for an Athenian *taxiarchos* is shown (twice), together with a shield decorated with a *gorgoneion*, in this depiction of the funeral of Patroclus and the sacrifice of Trojans shown on a volute crater decorated by the 'Darius Painter' (Trendall & Cambitoglou 1982: 495, 18/38; FR pl. 89) who probably worked in Tarentum, now in the National Archaeological Museum in Naples (3254). Dated to 340–320, this vase reflects the contemporary system of showing rank by the decoration of the helmet. (DEA/G. NIMATALLAH/Getty Images)

Finally, in ll.1173–74 of the *Peace* the chorus-leader refers to a *taxiarchos*, as well as wearing three crests, wearing a bright crimson cloak. Again, this might not be specific to holders of the rank of *taxiarchos*, but could have been thought of simply as a suitable 'military' colour to wear. This might have been under the influence of the Lacedaemonian army, which wore crimson, but it might simply have been thought of as dressing oneself in the best clothing available for battle. Xenophon tells us (*An.* 3.2.7) that he wore

Honorary decree (the text is lost) showing the war-god Ares crowning a figure, presumably a *stratēgos*, following a military victory he had won. Stylistically, the relief dates to the third quarter of the 4th century, following the reintroduction of the muscle-cuirass, which here is worn by Ares. At the right stands an unidentifiable goddess. The cloak of the honorand has been used as the basis for Plate E3. This artefact is held in Athens (National Museum 2947). (Author's photograph)

his finest clothes for battle, for, if the gods granted victory, it was appropriate to be wearing one's best attire to mark the occasion, or if he should die, it was also fitting to meet one's fate well dressed. Crimson was one of the most expensive dyes available, other than sea-purple, or saffron, which were beyond the means of ordinary citizens.

Starting with Pericles, it was the custom of the Athenian people to erect bronze statues to their *stratēgoi* showing them wearing Corinthian helmets. None of these statues has survived, but it was popular among the Roman elite to adorn their private houses with marble busts copying the heads from these statues. A quantity of such busts, featuring individuals all wearing Corinthian helmets and copied from originals stylistically dateable to the 4th century, have survived. In the absence of any inscriptions informing us who was the subject, despite the best efforts of scholars such as Jan Six and Poul Frederik Sigfred Poulsen, Director of the Ny Carlsberg Glyptotek, Copenhagen, the identity of the Athenian generals lying behind these portraits can only be guessed at.

Athenian archers

During the 5th century, as the revenues of empire grew, the Athenians made increasing use of their corps of archers, to supply each trireme

One of the most famous Roman copies of a head from a bronze statue of an Athenian general, identifiable as a *stratēgos* by his pushed-back Corinthian helmet, is the 'Pastoret Head', so called from one example formerly in the collection of the Marquis de Pastoret. This likeness is duplicated in several surviving copies of varying quality, this one in the Museo Nuovo dei Conservatori, Rome. Executed in Pentelic marble, it is usually dated to the first quarter of the 4th century on stylistic grounds, although it could well be later. It has been tentatively identified with a number of Athenian generals, including Conon, Phocion and Iphicrates, but certainty eludes us. (Bartosz Buszman)

Dated to *c*.420, this red-figure Attic *lekythos* by an unidentified artist and now in New York (MFA 56.171.58) bears a representation of Philoctetes on Lemnos. There are many versions of how the gods inflicted a festering wound in Philoctetes' foot. It smelt so bad that the Achaeans had to abandon him on the island of Lemnos while on their way to Troy. (Marie-Lan Nguyen/Wikimedia/CC BY 2.5)

Grave stele in Athens (National Museum 752), significantly from the Peiraeus, dating probably to the early 4th century and showing one Demokleides, son of Demetrios, seated on the prow of a trireme, on which he has lost his life serving in a naval battle. He sits on an *ephaptis* cloak. (Author's photograph)

E NAVAL PERSONNEL

The same citizens were called upon to fight in the fleet as in the land army.

(1) Naval archer

Representations of Greek archers, as opposed to Scythians, Persians and other foreigners, are quite rare in Athenian art. The majority portray figures from Greek mythology such as Odysseus or Philoctetes. These representations depict archery equipment in a remarkably uniform way. As this type of equipment was familiar to the artists, we can assume that it was used by Athenian archers. As the Athenians had no skills in bow-making, archery equipment had to be imported from the Black Sea area. It was not astronomically expensive. A bow and quiver worth 15 drachmas were offered as first prize and a bow worth 7 drachmas as second prize in a competition at Coresia on the island of Ceos in the early 3rd century (*IG* xii.5 647, 27–28). Nevertheless, as the archers must have been recruited from the poorer Athenians, we presume that they would have been supplied with their equipment.

The Scythian *gorytos* was a combined quiver and bow-case. In the Athenian examples, although of the same basic shape, the arrows only are kept inside the arrow-case. This was manufactured in two wooden halves covered with leather, to judge from the outside, which appears to be dappled ox-hide. We can see a frame running along the side and bottom of the case, holding the two halves together. The arrow-case was open at one end, where it was covered by a flap of material or leather. The bow, when not in use, was held by two straps on the outside of the arrow-case. The shape of the two arms of the Scythian bow were asymmetrical, as it was designed to be shot from horseback. The arrow-case was worn at the waist, in the Scythian way.

(2) Naval peltast

The crews of the triremes would increasingly be disembarked to fight as peltasts in the 4th century. This man carries a fighting spear as depicted on the *kōthon* from Stuttgart (see p.37), rather than javelins; Roman *velites* carried seven javelins.

(3) Naval hoplite

According to the 'Decree of Themistocles', moved when the Athenians decided to abandon Attica to the Persians, the number of fighting men aboard a trireme was 14, including four archers and ten young *epibatai* (Fornara 1977: no. 55). Literally, *epibatēs* means 'passenger', but the term is usually translated as 'marine'. Plutarch says (*Themistocles* 14.1) that at Salamis there were 18 fighting men per ship: four archers and 14 hoplites. In 426, during operations in Aetolia, the Athenians disembarked 300 *epibatai* from 30 ships (Thucydides, *Hist.* 3.95.2) together with archers (3.98.1). About 120 of the hoplites 'all of the same age, finished here, the best men in truth the city of Athens lost in this war' (3.98.4). The first fleet that was sent to Sicily consisted of 60 'swift' triremes with 700 *thetes* aboard as *epibatai*.

Around the middle of the 5th century, hoplite shield devices become confined to a narrow range of symbols, a star or a laurel wreath being the favourites. This shield is decorated with a star contained within a laurel wreath surrounded by a wave pattern, based on a jug in the Louvre (G 571) decorated by the 'Shuvalov Painter', active *c*.440–410. We have no idea what colours would be used. Shields could be decorated quite elaborately. According to Plutarch (*Nicias* 28.5), the shield of Nicias, who was very wealthy, was decorated in gold and purple interwoven with great skill. The days of hereditary shield devices were over. Plutarch tells us (*Alcib.* 16.1–2) that Alcibiades had made for himself a gilded shield bearing no ancestral device, but an Eros armed with a thunderbolt.

with its complement of four archers, and to provide garrisons and units for campaigns on land (Trundle 2010: 151–52). By the beginning of the Peloponnesian War, the corps of archers stood at 1,600. Most of these would have been recruited from the *thetes*, the poorer Athenian citizens. A monument for the dead of the tribe Erechtheis for 459 (*IG* i³ 1147, 67–70) lists four archers, who must have been citizens. The triremes of the fleet would be crewed by tribe. An inscription listing the members of the crews of the triremes includes citizen archers (*IG* i³ 1032, [47], 168). A casualty list of the tribe Aiantis lists Eukleides the *taxiarchos* and Isodikos the *toxarchos* (commander of archers) among the fallen (*IG* i³ 1186, 80), indicating that the *toxarchos* was a tribal appointment, like the *taxiarchos*. The [*tox*]*archoi* are also attested in an inscription dated to the 440s or early 430s (*IG* i³ 138, 13–14).

We also read of 'barbarian' archers. These are attested from the first half of the 5th century (*IG* i³ 1192, 152–57) and possibly in a list of similar date (*IG* i³ 1172, 35). Curiously, they appear in a list of Athenian citizens fallen from *c*.411 (*IG* i³ 1190, 136–37). Aristarchus, one of the leaders of 'The Four Hundred', fled Athens in 411 with 'some of the most barbarous of the archers' (Thucydides, *Hist.* 8.98.1).

Athenian peltasts

At the beginning of the Peloponnesian War the Athenians made use of foreign peltasts. In 425 the general Demosthenes was forced to arm the crews of his ships with whatever was to hand to bring about the surrender of the Lacedaemonian hoplites on the island of Sphacteria.

The first reference we get to *peripoloi* ('patrollers') is during the invasion of Megara in 424, when Thucydides mentions (*Hist.* 4.67.2) 'the Plataean *psiloi* and other *peripoloi*' led by Demosthenes, fresh from his successes at Sphacteria. The 'other *peripoloi*' also seem to have been foreigners. Phrynichus, one of 'The Four Hundred', was assassinated by 'a man of the *peripoloi*' due to a plot hatched by those who met in the 'house of the *peripolarchos*' (Thucydides, *Hist.* 8.92.2) among whom were an Argive, an Aetolian from Calydon and a Megarian. So, the probability is that foreigners, most probably largely political exiles and opposed to non-democratic forms of government, continued to serve in the Athenian *peripoloi* in 411. This force would have been commanded by Athenians. Shortly afterwards we are told that the pro-oligarchic general Alexikles was arrested by Aristocrates the *taxiarchos*, assisted by the Athenian Hermon, one of the *peripoloi*, the commander of those stationed in Mounychia (Thucydides, *Hist.* 8.92.5). From this reference we can conclude that there were several detachments of *peripoloi* stationed in different forts in Attica. There might, however, have been only one *peripolarchos*, presumably an officer elected by the Athenian state.

Later in 424 the Athenians carried out a full levy (*pendēmei*) of the Athenians themselves, of the metics, and also of such foreigners (*xenoi*) as were present in the city (Thucydides, *Hist.* 4.90.1), which was sent into Boeotia. A passage in Thucydides dealing with the ensuing battle of Delium is most revealing:

> There were no regularly armed *psiloi* present, nor did there happen to be any in the city. And those who had joined in, though they were many times greater than their enemy, had mostly come unarmed,

because there had been a levy [*panstratia*] of *xenoi* as well as *astoi* [town-dwellers], and thus as soon as they made a start for home, they were not present but for a few. (*Hist.* 4.94.1)

In 409, the Athenians resolved that Thrasyllus might mobilize 1,000 hoplites, 100 cavalry and 50 triremes (Xenophon, *Hell.* 1.1.34). Thrasyllus took the ships which had been voted him and equipped 5,000 of his sailors so that he might employ them as peltasts (1.2.1), 100 per ship. He then sailed for Samos. A force from Miletus consisting of hoplites (as their shields were later used to construct a trophy) came up against them, and, finding the Athenian *psiloi* scattered, pursued them. Thereupon the peltasts and two *lochoi* of hoplites came to the aid of the Athenian *psiloi* and killed all but a few of the men of Miletus. A later section of the same passage mentions that the Athenian forces consisted of hoplites, cavalry, peltasts, *epibatai* and 'all the rest' (1.2.7).

So, it seems that shortly after the battle of Delium a decision was made to train the poorer Athenians who supplied the oarsmen for the Athenian fleet as peltasts. This training must have taken place during the second year of the *ephēbeia*. Subsequently, we regularly read of Athenian peltasts being used, not only in naval contexts but on land also. The first certain reference to Athenian peltasts in use on land was when in 379 the Lacedaemonians sent out an army under Cleombrotus to bring the Thebans to submission following their expulsion of the Lacedaemonian garrison. The Athenians, we are told, dispatched Chabrias to guard the road that led through Eleutherae with 'the peltasts of the Athenians' (Xenophon, *Hell.* 5.4.14).

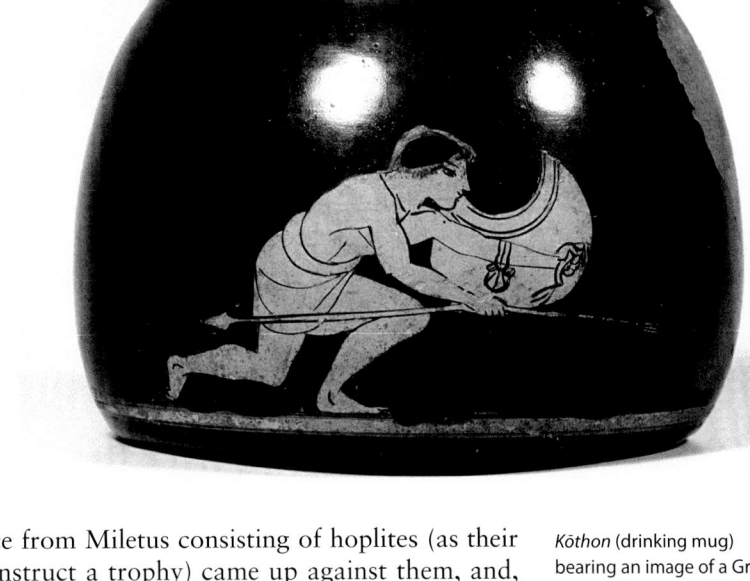

Kōthon (drinking mug) bearing an image of a Greek peltast. This is a problematic representation, by an unidentified artist, dating to about the middle of the 5th century, but it is the only surviving representation of a Greek, presumably Athenian, peltast. He carries a wood-and-leather shield, called a *peltē*, which is defined by Aristotle as a shield without a rim (unlike the hoplite shield). It was probably fitted with a bronze handle into which the left forearm fitted, and a rope handle grasped by the left hand. He carries a single short, thin, double-headed spear, more like a fighting spear than a javelin. He wears an *ephaptis* wrapped round his waist. (Landesmuseum Württemberg, Inv. No. 4.136)

The Sicilian Expedition

In 415, the Athenians decided to send an expedition to Sicily that proved disastrous. At least one reason for the disaster was the unclear command structure. Since the administrative changes of 487/86, unlinking the *stratēgoi* from command of the tribal *phylai*, overall command was vested in one *stratēgos* or shared among several who exercised collegiate authority (Crowley 2012: 35). For example, according to Diodorus Siculus (*Hist.* 13.97.6 cf. 106.1), each of the *stratēgoi* present with the fleet in 406 held the supreme command in turn for one day at a time.

The Athenians decided to send to Sicily 60 ships with Alcibiades, Nicias and Lamachus, each of whom was designated as *stratēgos autokratoros* ('general possessing full powers'; Thucydides, *Hist*. 6.8.2, 26.1), which is a contradiction in terms. In his reportage of the divisive speeches that were exchanged, Nicias accused Alcibiades of being too young to hold command (Thucydides, *Hist*. 6.12.2), but in fact we do not know whether there was any minimum age at which the *stratēgeia* could be held (30 was the minimum age for councillors and jurymen).

The initial number of hoplites mobilized from the *katologos* was 1,500 (Thucydides, *Hist*. 6.43). They were subsequently joined by another 1,200 Athenian hoplites 'of the best class from the *katalogos*' under Demosthenes (Thucydides, *Hist*. 7.20–27). This is a puzzling reference to how the hoplite *katalogos* was drawn up.

The *katalogoi*

We do not know precisely the way in which the *katalogoi*, the 'muster-rolls' of people who had to turn up for a campaign, were compiled. Demosthenes tells us (*Against Polycles* 50.6) that in the case of a naval campaign, it was the *bouleutai* and the *dēmarchoi* who should prepare the *katalogoi* of the demesmen. At the beginning of the year, the *bouleutai* had been responsible for carrying out the *dokimasia* of the cavalrymen, deciding who was fit to serve. They drew up the *katologos* of cavalrymen for each tribe, in conjunction with the *phylarchoi*, which were then passed on to the *hipparchoi* who operated out of an office called the *hipparcheion* (IG ii² 895, 6). In turn the *bouleutai* had to inform the *dēmarchoi* which of the demesmen had been admitted to the cavalry and should not be included when they drew up the hoplite *katologos*. The hoplite *katologos* would be drawn up by the *taxiarchos* of each tribe in conjunction with the *dēmarchoi* (Pollux, *On*. 8.115), each of whom would have the *lexiarchicon grammateion*, the list of all the citizens available for military service in his deme at his disposal. The *taxiarchos* would then lodge the hoplite *katalogos* for his tribal regiment in the *stratēgeion* in the agora, which the *stratēgoi* shared jointly.

This picture is confirmed by a speech of Lysias (*Alcib*. 15.5) in which it is reported that Alcibiades the Younger avoided hoplite service by convincing Pamphilos, his *phylarchos*, to persuade the *taxiarchos* of his tribe to erase Alcibiades' name from the hoplite *katalogos*. Alcibiades was to have served in the *hippotoxotai* under Pamphilos, but never turned up.

When the tribal *katalogoi* were published, appeals could be lodged against illegal mobilization with the *stratēgos* responsible (Crowley 2012: 28–29). One cause of appeal could be if an individual had already performed military service that year. In a speech written for Polyaenus (Lysias, *For the Soldier* 9.4), the latter complains that he had not been at home for two months when he was enrolled once again as a soldier. Polyaenus, one notes, was threatened with loss of citizenship.

F **JAVELIN-THROWING FROM HORSEBACK COMPETITION**
Xenophon emphasized (*Hipparchikos* 1.6, 12; *Mem*. 3.3.7) that one of the duties of the *hipparchos* was to train as many men as possible to throw the javelin from horseback. The competition called 'javelin-throwing from horseback' (*af'hippou akuntizonti*) is mentioned by Xenophon (*Hipp*. 1.26) and in an inscription dating to the early 4th century (*IG* ii² 2311, 68–70). The competition is also recorded on seven Attic vases, the oldest dating to 415–405 (Sparkes 1977: 11), some of them recording victory in the Panathenaic Games. The young cavalrymen were very particular about their appearance and took pride in it. Long hair was very fashionable, as it was at Lacedaemon, with whose political system the young men sympathized. They had extremely rich parents, capable of supporting the upkeep of a horse, which had no use in agriculture before the horse-collar reached Europe in Byzantine times; and they could afford the most expensive fashions.

Attic white-ground *lekythos* in Athens (National Archaeological Museum 12275), painted by the 'Reed Painter' (Beazley 1963: 1377, 16), whose years of production spanned the years 420–400, showing a young horseman wearing a black cloak, which may mean that he is an *ephēbos*. His white tunic is of a thick blanket-weave material, decorated with two lines of extended green rectangles at the shoulder and at the hip. It is difficult to decide if this young man is wearing a tan, felt *petasos* hat, or a bronze helmet of similar shape. (Author's photograph)

The resulting *katologos* was posted up on the Monument to the Ten Eponymous Heroes in the Athenian agora (see p.63) below the statue of the tribe's tutelary hero, probably drawn up by deme, most probably on whitened boards written on in ink. Aristophanes asserted that the *taxiarchoi*

> enter some of our names on the lists and erase others, higgledy-piggledy, two or three times. The expedition sets out tomorrow, and the man's bought no provisions, because he didn't know he was going on it – and then he stops in front of the statue of Pandion and sees his name, and rushes off in distress, with a curdling look in his eyes because of his misfortune. They do that to us country folk – not so much to the townspeople. (*Peace* 1180–86)

In the *Knights*, Aristophanes' impersonified *dēmos* declares that 'no hoplite whose name is entered on the *katalogos* is to get it transferred to another list by improper influence; it shall remain entered where it was originally' (1369–70).

Looking at the evidence for the Sicilian mobilization, Christ (2001: 402) concluded that the *stratēgoi* chose individuals who were judged to be particularly suitable. Perhaps he goes too far in positing that once those known personally or recommended to the expedition leaders and their subordinates had been selected, they may have drawn 'more or less randomly' from the pool of able-bodied manpower (Christ 2001: 402). It can hardly have been as random as that.

One obvious way to bring order to the mobilization procedure, if a general levy was not required, was to draw up the *katologos* by age-group (*eph'hēlikias*). Aeschines (*Emb.* 2.168) states that he had frequently performed military service by age-group. Demosthenes calls as a witness in his speech *Against Meidias* (21.95) one Straton of Phaleron who had served in all the expeditions by age-group for which he had been called up.

Oligarchic regimes at Athens

In all, 2,700 hoplites were sent to Sicily. Few of them, however, would return. In the wake of the disastrous expedition, in the autumn of 413 the Athenians appointed a committee of ten *probouloi* from men over 40 years old 'to prepare measures with reference to the present situation' (*AP* 29.2). I have suggested (Sekunda 2016) that this might be the occasion on which the mounted torch-race (*aphippolampada*) at the Bendideia was introduced, and it could also be when the 'javelin-throwing from horseback' competition was introduced into the Panathenaic Games. These measures might have strengthened the group cohesion among the young men (*neaniskoi*) of the Athenian *hippeis* to such an extent that the oligarchic regime of 'The Four Hundred' was able to seize power two years later thanks, largely, to their support.

The first and only reference to the mounted torch-race at Athens comes in Plato's *Republic* (327–28), of which the dramatic date is probably 413/12, which mentions that the competition took place for the first time at the festival in honour of the goddess Artemis Bendis. The mounted torch-race

An uninscribed Attic relief in London (British Museum 2155), perhaps dating to the beginning of the 4th century, shows Bendis (right) standing in front of two cloaked figures and eight naked athletes wearing headbands. Only the first figure carries a torch, which supports the statement of Plato that the competition was a relay race. The relief presumably shows the victorious tribal team. One of the cloaked figures standing in front is presumably the *phylarchos* of the tribal squadron; the other might be a *gymnasiarchos*. (Author's photograph)

may not long have survived the fall of 'The Four Hundred'; it is not recorded outside Plato; nor is it illustrated by any archaeological object except for the relief illustrated here.

The regime of 'The Four Hundred', which ruled for less than four months, paved the way for 'The Five Thousand'. Thucydides implies that 'The Five Thousand' were drawn from 'all who could furnish themselves with a hoplite's equipment' (*Hist.* 8.107.1). According to a speech written for the eldest son of Polystratos, who had been appointed to draw up the catalogue of 'The Five Thousand' by 'The Four Hundred', Polystratos, rather than stick to the original figure of 5,000, entered 9,000 names – 'anyone who wished to be included' – on the list (Lysias, *On the Murder of Eratosthenes* 20.13). No one was to receive pay for any office. Thucydides rates it as the best government the Athenians ever had 'at least in my time' (*Hist.* 8.97.2), but it lasted less than ten months. The Athenians in the city made peace with the democratic fleet in Samos and fought the war to its end in 404, following which the regime of 'The Thirty Tyrants' took power, only to fall a year later.

Because of their shape, scenes on vases of 'The Talcott Class', a type of narrow-necked jug, are best viewed 'rolled out'. This example is in Athens (National Museum 1631). The painter of this jug has not been identified, but on stylistic grounds it was painted *c*.400. I would have thought that the 'Painter of the Chubby Horses' would be appropriate. The rider on the left has still to throw his javelin, his right hand poised to cast. The rider on the right has thrown: his right arm still extended, his javelin bounces off the shield, of which the target area is indicated by a wreath. He has won, because he is shown already crowned. Beneath the shield lies a broken javelin, left by a previous unsuccessful competitor. (Natalia Kozłowska)

Detail of the gravestone of Panaitios of the deme of Hamaxantia in Athens (National Museum 884; *IG*^{2} 5601) dating to the first quarter of the 4th century, the large slab being re-used to cover a canal in front of the city wall in the Kerameikos. He is quite probably related to Panaitios, *hipparchos* in 425/24. The baggy overfall of the tunic is typical for the period. Note the combination of the long cavalry spear, with its small leaf-shaped head and long spear-butt, and the pair of rather heavy javelins. (Wojciech Brillowski)

ATHENIAN FORCES 404–362

Cavalry

Athenian representations of cavalrymen from the first third of the 4th century, whether on tombstones or in mythological scenes on pottery, depict cavalrymen equipped with a combination of two javelins and a distinctively long combat spear. This is identical to the hoplite spear in appearance and, apart from during combat with enemy cavalry, gave the range required by the mounted cavalryman to strike down an enemy on foot. This reflects an important role of Athenian cavalry in the first stages of the Peloponnesian War, namely to limit the ability of the invading Peloponnesian hoplite infantry to disperse and ravage crops, for fear of being attacked out of formation by Athenian cavalry (Spence 1990). The spear must have been rather unwieldy

Detail of a *pelike* (storage jar) from Tanagra now in Athens (National Museum 1333), decorated by an artisan 'Near the Pronomos Painter' (Beazley 1963: 1337,8) *c*.400–390. Castor or Pollux attacks a giant on foot. The spear-butt is cut off by the upper edge of the central scene, but note the pair of javelins shown behind the horse's head, probably held in the crook of the left arm, leaving the left hand free to manage the reins. (Author's photograph)

when used against enemy cavalry, against whom the two javelins would be used in preference. This is reflected in a passage in Xenophon's *On Horsemanship*, written *c*.367, in which he describes a training exercise for the cavalry in the combined use of the cavalry spear (*dory*) and javelins as follows. First, the cavalry men pair off:

> one flies on his horse over all kinds of ground and retreats, reversing his spear so that it points backwards, while the other pursues, having buttons on his javelins and holding his spear in the same position, and when he gets within javelin shot, tries to hit the fugitive with the

Detail from 'The Great Melos Amphora' by the 'Suessula Painter' (Beazley 1963: 1344,1) painted *c*.400 or shortly thereafter, now in Paris (Louvre, S 1677), showing a battle between gods and giants (after Adolf Furtwängler, *Griechische Vasenmalerei*, 1904–32, pl. 96–97). Our figure, either Castor or Pollux, demonstrates how the fighting spear (*kamax*) was used against infantrymen, with a rapid downward thrust of the small leaf-shaped head. Note the bronze spear-butt. (Author's photograph)

blunted weapons, and if he gets near enough to use his spear, strikes his captive with it. (8.10)

In this passage Xenophon uses the generic Greek word for spear (*dory*), but there are reasons for believing this distinctively long spear might have been called, perhaps informally, a *kamax*. Principally, this word was applied to any type of wooden pole, but typically alongside *charax* to describe the long, thin vine props. In a number of the ancient Greek *lexica*, *kamax* is listed alongside other words for spear and is defined as 'a cavalry spear' or a 'straight pike'. Euripides, the contemporary Athenian tragedian, twice uses the word *kamax* to mean spear (*Hecuba* 1155; *El.* 852).

Doubts have been expressed on whether the list of *hippeis* who fell at the battles of Coroneia and Nemea in 394/93 (*IG* ii² 5222) includes all Athenian cavalrymen lost that year, or just those of the tribe Akamantis, bearing in mind the list contains just 12 names. It was probably, in fact, a list of all the *hippeis* who fell that year, as cavalry service was far safer than hoplite service. In an account of his military service, Mantitheus stated that in operations

Found west of Athens, in the area of the state burial ground (*dēmosion sēma*), this *epistylos*, or crowning element in the shape of an *anthemion* (honeysuckle) of the official monument listing the *hippeis* who fell at the battles of Coroneia and Nemea in the Corinthia during the archonship of Euboulides (394/93), is now in Athens (National Museum 754). The inscription (*IG* ii² 5222; Harding 1985: no. 19B) runs: 'These cavalrymen died at Corinth: The *phylarchos* Antiphanes, Melesias, Onetorides, Lysitheos, Pandios, Nikomachos, Theangelos, Phanes, Demokles, Dexileos, Endelos. At Coronea: Neokleides'. (Wojciech Brillowski)

against the Lacedaemonian garrison at Haliartos he had been enrolled by Orthobulus (presumably his *phylarchos*) for service in the cavalry, but seeing

> that it was everyone's opinion that, whereas the cavalry were assured of safety, the infantry would have to face danger; so, while the others mounted on horseback illegally, without having passed the *dokimasia*, I went up to Orthobulus and told him to strike me off the *katologos*, as I thought it shameful, while the majority were to face danger, to take the field with precaution for my own safety. (Lysias, *Mant*. 16.13)

The *prodromoi*

The last time we read of the Athenian horse-archers was during operations carried out against the Lacedaemonian garrison in Haliartos in 395, in which Alcibiades the Younger participated as a horse-archer (Lysias, 14, 15). The *prodromoi* or 'scouts' were a branch of the Athenian cavalry raised in the winter of 395/94 to replace the horse-archers, who were disbanded after

Also found west of Athens is the right half of the *epistylos* in Pentelic marble (National Museum 2744) of an inscription (*IG* ii² 5221; Harding 1985: 19A) reading: '[Of the Athenians the following] died at Corinth and in Boeotia'. Five tribal names can be read in the single line of the inscription preserved below the *epistylos*. The two hoplites represent the Athenian fallen, and the attacking cavalryman is probably a Boeotian, wearing an early form of the Boeotian helmet. Note his animal-hilted sabre. Three similar figures presumably adorned the other half: the tail of a horse is just visible on the left of the remaining relief. (Wojciech Brillowski)

Relief of Dexileos in Pentelic marble from a family grave-plot (*temenos*) in the Kerameikos cemetery and now in Kerameikos Museum (P 1130). It was erected by the family in his honour, although he was buried in the state burial ground, which this relief faces. He is depicted triumphing over death, thrusting downwards towards an enemy hoplite. The shaft of the lance would have been added in bronze: small holes are visible in the marble to secure it. Note the sword belt and the small lead weights at the corners of the cloak. (Sp!ros/Wikimedia/ CC BY-SA 3.0)

the battle of Haliartos. The *prodromoi* took on the duties of scouts and couriers previously performed by the horse-archers. The inscription below the relief of Dexileos (*IG* ii² 6217; Harding 1985: no. 19.C) implies they were internally recruited from among the tribal cavalry regiments:

> Dexileos, son of Lysanios, from Thorikos,
> was born in the archonship of Teisandros [414/13],
> died in the archonship of Euboulides [394/93]
> at Corinth, one of the five cavalrymen.

One way of interpreting this passage is that each *phylē* of cavalry selected five of its best men to serve as *prodromoi*, so each *hipparchos* would have a small troop of 25 *prodromoi* at his disposal. This is demonstrated by a passage in Xenophon (*Hipp* 1.25) suggesting that to induce a spirit of competition among the *phylarchoi*, the *hipparchos* should take care that the *prodromoi*

'around him' should be armed as well as possible and be constantly trained in the javelin.

According to the *Athēniaōn Politeia*, the *boulē* held a scrutiny of the *prodromoi*, 'to see which men appear capable of serving, and if it rejects anyone his service is at an end' (49.1). One of the skills in which they were tested was throwing the javelin from horseback. This passage demonstrates that the institution of the *prodromoi* lasted until the end of democracy, and implies they were paid at that time. The *prodromoi* are attested at Athens well into the 3rd century (Schäfer 2019: 44–45).

Xenophon reminds the *phylarchoi* that they are entitled to arm the men in accordance with the regulations, compelling the men to pay for their arms afterwards 'as the law ordains' (*Hipp.* 1.23). As much attention was paid to the turnout of the cavalry on parades as was devoted to their performance on campaign. Demosthenes tells us (*First Philippic* 4.35) that as much money was spent annually on the Panathenaic and other festivals as would be required to fit out a naval expedition. One would expect the *prodromoi*, then, to put on quite a show.

The *phylai* of cavalry could operate independently. We hear of 'The Thirty' sending two *phylai* against their democratic adversaries (Xenophon, *Hell.* 2.4.4). Xenophon recommends (*Hipp.* 2.2–6) that each *phylē* of cavalry was drawn up in files ten ranks deep, at the head of which would be stationed a *dekadarchos* ('commander of ten'), selected from among the keenest men. The rear rank of the file would be commanded by a *pempadarchos* (cf. 4.9), a 'commander of five', chosen from the oldest and most sensible men. Xenophon emphasizes (*Hipp.* 8.17) that the files should be of an even number, to make it possible to halve the regiment into two *taxeis*. Many regiments were well below the establishment strength of 100 men, and it was more important to preserve the depth of the file and half-file, rather than the frontage of the regiment. These arrangements were probably borrowed from current practice in the Lacedaemonian cavalry.

Down to the 360s, Athenian cavalrymen tend to be depicted wearing either *petasos* hats or helmets. Some are shown wearing cuirasses and some not. It would be tempting to identify those without body armour as all *prodromoi*, but Athenian cavalrymen of the line might have avoided wearing the cuirass for reasons of comfort. The type of cuirass shown tends to be a muscle-cuirass, similar to those used in the 5th century, without groin-flaps.

LEFT
One face of an altar in Athens (National Museum 3708) stylistically dated to the early 4th century shows a *hippeus* wearing a muscle-cuirass, boots, tunic, cloak and a *petasos* hat, perched on the crown of his head, riding down a hoplite, who has lost his *pilos*. (Francesco Bini/Wikimedia/CC BY-SA 4.0)

CENTRE
This, central, scene shows a lightly clad horseman, probably a *prodromos* (note the sword-hilt and boots), riding down an Arcadian peltast of the new 'Iphicratean' type, which dates the scene to some unrecorded clash of the 360s. ((Francesco Bini/Wikimedia/CC BY-SA 4.0)

RIGHT
The third face shows a horseman without a cuirass riding down an unhelmed hoplite clad in an *exomis* tunic and armed with a short sword. (Francesco Bini/Wikimedia/CC BY-SA 4.0)

Occasionally, monuments show the Corinthian helmet still in use with the new muscle-cuirass. It is possible that this very traditional style of helmet was still worn as a badge of rank by the *stratēgoi*, for busts depicting Athenian generals in the 4th century invariably show the *stratēgoi* wearing such headgear. This example in Copenhagen (IN 1508), acquired in Athens in 1896, has been dated along stylistic lines to the 330s. (Marie-Lan Nguyen/Wikimedia/CC BY 4.0)

Infantry reforms of the 360s

From the 360s onwards, Athenian state revenue began to grow again, principally because of an increase in activity in the silver mines of Laurium. Military reform became financially viable once more and started to enter the political debate. In the latter half of the 4th century, Attic funerary monuments show that Athenian infantry had started to wear cuirasses again, specifically the muscle-cuirass. We can probably connect this with a passage in Plutarch (*Mor.* 193f) recording a quip made by the Theban general Epaminondas on hearing that the Athenians had sent an army into the Peloponnese decked out with new equipment, who is reported to have said: 'Why should Antigenes cry if Tellen has a new flute or two?' Plutarch explains: 'Tellen was the worst of flute players, and Antigenes the best.' Athenians started to send armies into the Peloponnese against the Thebans as early as the spring of 369, but the reference probably relates to Epaminondas' final invasion of the Peloponnese in 362. It is possible that heavy body armour had been reintroduced into Greek warfare by the Thebans, along with their new tactics of attack in depth.

In the 360s, Athenian funerary reliefs start to show hoplites wearing muscle-cuirasses and 'Phrygian' helmets. The muscle-cuirass is of the same shape as that worn by the Athenian cavalry earlier in the century, with a projection at the bottom edge covering the abdomen, except that the cuirass now has a couple of hinged bronze flaps at the shoulder. Sometimes the cuirass is worn with groin-flaps, probably in examples of a later date. The impression we get from the funerary monuments is not one of uniformity. The muscle-cuirass is universal, but there is a large diversity in the arrangement of the groin-flaps and the shape of the shoulder-guards. The Phrygian helmet dominates, but older types are represented, such as the old-fashioned Attic shaped helmets, and the occasional Boeotian helmet may be retained by a former cavalryman, compelled because of his advancing age to serve in the infantry. Nevertheless, some type of enabling legislation must have existed to force the adoption of the muscle-cuirass on the Athenian citizenry who served in the infantry. We are reminded of the passage in Xenophon's *Hipparchikos* (1.23) cited above in which he reminds the *phylarchoi* that they are entitled to arm the men in accordance with the regulations, compelling the men to pay for their arms afterwards 'as the law ordains'.

Cavalry reforms of the 360s

After his return from exile *c.*367, and probably on the eve of the outbreak of war with Thebes in 365, Xenophon produced two pamphlets: the *Hipparchikos*, which outlined the duties of the *hipparchoi* recommending reform in cavalry tactics; and *On Horsemanship*, recommending changes in equipment.

The final, twelfth, chapter of *On Horsemanship* constitutes a kind of 'appendix' to the work as a whole. This part, at least, of the pamphlet appeared after the *Hipparchikos*, for at 12.14 Xenophon mentions the latter work. He recommends improvements to be made in the equipment of the Athenian cavalry. These include the adoption of the Boeotian helmet, which 'affords the best protection to all the parts that project above the breastplate without obstructing the sight'. I imagine that the Athenian cavalry had adopted the Boeotian helmet by 362, and this was the reason why the

Detail of a marble *loutrophoros* (vase) showing Polystratos, son of Philopolis (Athens, National Museum, 3473). It is generally assumed that this Polystratos is a grandson of an earlier Polystratos active in 410/09, and so this relief is usually dated to the 390s. There is no reason why our Polystratos should not belong to a later generation of the same family, however, and the date in the 360s would fill the other archaeological evidence much better. Red colouring is preserved on the tunics and *ephaptis* cloak. Behind Polystratos stands a juvenile carrying the rest of his equipment. (Marsyas/Wikimedia/CC BY 2.5)

Theban horse who opposed them at the battle of Mantineia painted their helmets white to identify themselves in the mêlée (Xenophon, *Hell.* 7.5.20).

Xenophon also recommends (*Hipp.* 5.13) that the city should acquire a force of *hamippoi*, and (9.7) that that they should be recruited from foreigners who are very bitter against the enemy. *Hamippoi* were trained to run alongside the cavalry, holding onto the tails of the horses, and the hems of the riders' cloaks. In the mêlée they would attack horse and rider alike with daggers and other weapons. A favourite trick was to slip underneath the enemy horse and rip its belly open with a dagger. Service in the *hamippoi* was evidently not for the faint-hearted.

It seems that the Athenian state was fast to act on Xenophon's recommendations, for Diodorus Siculus tells us (*Hist.* 15.85.4) that at the battle of Mantineia the Athenian cavalry on the left flank were defeated by their Theban opponents, not because of their inferior mounts or horsemanship, but because of the better equipment and better tactical use of the *psiloi* fighting for the Thebans. This implies that *hamippoi* were present on the Athenian side. Subsequently, the Athenians seem to have maintained a force of *hamippoi* on a permanent basis, for according to the *Athēniaōn Politeia*, the *boulē* held an annual scrutiny of the *hamippoi* 'and if it rejects anyone that is the end of his paid service' (49.1).

Xenophon describes (*Hipp.* 3.10–13) a cavalry competition called the *anthippasia* held in front of the *boulē* and assembled citizens in the 'hippodrome' at Athens, the whereabouts of which are not precisely known. The cavalry was divided into two groups of five *phylai*, each group led by one of the two *hipparchoi*, and demonstrated, at the trumpet blast, manoeuvres such as the charge, the halt, wheel round and charge again. A prize was awarded to the *phylē* who performed these manoeuvres best.

This anthropomorphic cheek-piece from a Phrygian helmet is of very similar shape to that shown on the *loutrophoros* of Polystratos. (Saint-Germain-en-Laye, Musée d'archéologie nationale, 4764)

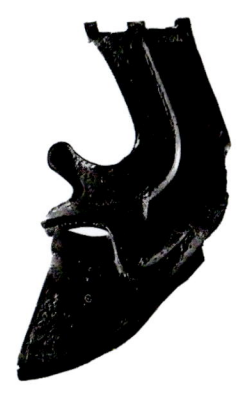

Fragment of a broken relief in Athens (Agora Museum I 7167) commemorating a victory in the *anthippasia* competition won by the tribe Leontis, third quarter of the 4th century. The relief would probably have originally contained five horses, and the *phylarchos* would have been shown on the right at the head of the file of five horses. The mature bearded figure shown on the extreme right, possibly a *pempadarchos*, is probably wearing a Boeotian helmet and armed with a sword with its hilt in the shape of the head of an animal or bird. (George E. Koronaios/Wikimedia/CC BY-SA 4.0)

Service 'in the divisions'

From the beginning, the tribal *taxeis* could be called upon to operate independently. In an inscription (*IG* i³ 1353; Fornara 1977: no. 101) relating to an expedition to Megara in 446, one Pythion of Megara states that he rescued three Athenian tribes – Pandionis, Kekropis and Antiochis – and led them to safety. The Athenian army was under pressure from many directions at the time, and it is highly probable that these three *taxeis* were detached from an army that had been mobilized previously (cf. Diodorus Siculus, *Hist.* 12.7; Plutarch, *Per.* 22.1–3; Thucydides, *Hist.* 1.114.1–115.1) for which, it seems, only three *taxeis* were tasked. It seems more likely that they were detached from a force already levied, rather than mobilized separately for the campaign.

In the middle of the 4th century, however, we start to hear of service 'in the divisions'. Aeschines states that his first service 'in the divisions' (*Emb.* 2.168) was in 366, escorting provisions to Phleious. The concept of service 'in the divisions' is best exemplified by Diodorus Siculus, who comments that on the outbreak of the Lamian War in 323, the Athenian assembly voted 'that all Athenians up to their fortieth year should be mobilized and that three *phylai* should guard Attica and that the other seven should be ready for campaign beyond the frontiers' (*Hist.* 18.10.2). The seven *phylai* were despatched, but the other three were presumably not mobilized yet, but held in reserve. When in 322 the Macedonian general Micion landed near Rhamnous, the *stratēgos* Phocion was able to lead the remaining three *phylai* against them (Plutarch, *Phocion* 27.1). So, the idea of mobilization 'in the divisions' seems to have been that only a proportion of the tribal *taxeis* would be sent out on campaign at any one time, to avoid the complete absence of age-groups over long periods.

Dated on stylistic lines to around the mid-4th century, this Athenian funerary marble *lekythos* is dedicated to a cavalryman, Kephisodotos, son of Konon of the deme Aithalidai, who almost certainly died in this campaign (Athens, National Archaeological Museum 3620). He is shown riding down a hoplite with a heifer's head as a shield device. This device was the badge of the Euboean League (see Sekunda & McBride 1986: 55–56), so Kephisodotos certainly died in battle fighting Euboean infantry, and the campaign of 349 is the only one in which we know the Athenian cavalry took part. (Hellenic National Archaeological Museum © Hellenic Ministry of Culture)

FROM MANTINEIA TO CHAERONEA (362–338)

Athenian *epilektoi*

Epilektoi, or 'picked troops', were citizen troops paid to be permanently available; hence they were better trained than the citizen troops that were mobilized. The problem was finding the financial resources to maintain them. One such band of *epilektoi* were the Arcadian *epariti*, 'those [who have been] counted out', of whom we first read in 369/68. They were paid out of the plundered treasures of Zeus at Olympia (Xenophon, *Hell*. 7.4.33). Athenian *epilektoi* are first mentioned in 349 at the battle of Tamynae. Though there is no evidence to prove the point, we may perhaps assume that, as in other Greek states, maintenance was provided to enable them to serve. Aeschines (*Emb*. 2.169) served in the *epilektoi* at Tamynae (presumably as an officer), where he won a crown for bravery. This is the first time *epilektoi* appear in the surviving sources, and as Athenian *epilektoi* are not mentioned in any account of the battle of Mantineia in 362, they must have been created at some time in between the two battles.

Xenophon proposes reform of the *ephēbeia*

In his treatise on *Revenues*, which appeared *c.*355, Xenophon suggests how the revenues of the Athenian state could be increased, positing that the Athenians could become better in obedience, better in orderliness and better in military effectiveness 'for two reasons' (meaning the two years of the *ephēbeia*): 'Those assigned to undergo physical exercise would do this much more diligently if receiving in the *gymnasia* a subsistence allowance [*trophē*] higher than that in the torch races, under the *gymnasiarchoi*' (4.52). Thus far, Xenophon is referring to the first year of the *ephēbeia*, in which the *ephēbos* was subject to physical training in the *gymnasia* in preparation for the torch-races. The remainder of the passage refers to the second year: 'and those assigned to guard duty in the forts [*phrouria*] and those assigned to peltast service [*peltazein*] and to patrolling [*peripolein*] in the countryside would do these things better with the subsistence allowance being distributed in recognition of each of the tasks'. The clear indication of this passage is that at the time of writing, those who could afford to equip themselves as hoplites served their second year in the forts, and those who could not do so served their second year equipped as peltasts patrolling the countryside. The peltasts must have been Athenian citizens if they received a subsistence allowance. If they were non-citizens then they would have received pay (*misthos*).

G   THE BATTLE OF TAMYNAE

In this plate both cavalrymen are shown riding bareback (cavalrymen are shown riding bareback in the Parthenon frieze). Proper saddles only came into use in the Roman period, but prior to that the saddlecloth (*ephippios*) had gradually come into use, at first in the Achaemenid Empire, and then among the Greeks and the other peoples that were living near it. When the confiscated property of the *hermokopidai*, the people accused of mutilating the herms (sculptures) of Athens before the Sicilian expedition set sail from the city in 415, was auctioned off, among the items sold were two saddlecloths belonging to Alcibiades. Meritt (1984: 95) has pointed out that there are no representations of saddlecloths either in vase-paintings or in sculpture of the Greek mainland before the end of the 5th century. He believes that Alcibiades, fond of luxury and extravagance, was living ahead of his time in acquiring these saddlecloths as well as other imports from Miletus, for example, which are recorded among his possessions. Meritt also points out that Xenophon in his *On Horsemanship* (7.5), published *c*.369–65, when dealing with the question of how one should seat oneself on a horse, says that whether riding bareback, or seated on an *ephippios*, one should not ride as if sitting on a chair, but should grip the horse with one's thighs, and adopt an upright stance which will allow the rider to throw his javelin and deliver a blow from horseback with more force.

Antiphanes was an Athenian comic poet whose first play was staged *c*.383. In a fragment of his play *Hippeis* preserved in Athenaeus (*Deip.* 11.503a), the *hippeis* were forced to use their *ephipipoi* as coverings for the dinner-couch: presumably in the field. He also mentions that they were compelled to use their beautiful *piloi* as *kadoi*. *Kados* was a Greek word normally used for 'bucket', in this context for containing wine. We can add this to the reference in Aristophanes to a *phlyarchos* eating *alphita* from his *pilos*: in both cases the *piloi* could not have been made out of felt, but must have been made of bronze.

(1) *Hamippos*

The details of the dress and equipment worn by this figure are indistinct, but a dagger in the right hand, and a baldrick (cross belt) running from the right shoulder, can be made out. This would presumably have carried the scabbard of the dagger. He is probably wearing a conical felt cap, a *pilos*, rather than a bronze helmet of the same shape.

(2) *Prodromos*

Cephisodorus probably served in the Athenian *prodromoi*, as he is unarmoured apart from his Boeotian helmet in plain bronze. He wears a cloak, tunic and riding boots. A sword belt is slung over his right shoulder.

(3) Cavalryman

This figure is based on a number of sources, the most important of which is an Athenian marble funerary *lekythos* (EMA 2586). The central figure shows a warrior equipped with a spear, which was originally painted on the sculpture; a Boeotian helmet; a muscle-cuirass with shoulder-flaps and two rows of groin-flaps; and a tunic and cloak. From the second quarter of the 4th century, cavalry were increasingly used to fight cavalry, rather than unformed infantry, and this made necessary a change in the type of spear used. By the second quarter of the century the traditional cavalry spear had been replaced by another model, called a *xyston*, or 'whittled' spear. It was used by the Macedonian cavalry at the battle of the Granicus in 334. Plutarch mentions (*Life of Alexander* 16.11) that at the battle of Granicus, Kleitos 'the Black' saved the life of Alexander by killing the Persian Rhoisakes with his *xyston*. In his account of the battle, Arrian tells us (*Anabasis of Alexander* 1.15.5–8) that the Macedonian cavalrymen were getting the better of the battle because they were fighting with cornel-wood *xysta* against the *paltai* of the Persians. At this point in the battle, Alexander's spear was broken. He called on Aretas, one of the royal grooms, to hand over his spear, but Aretas had broken his lance and was fighting on with the broken half. Shortly after, Alexander killed Spithridates by pushing his *xyston* through the Persian's cuirass. Then, Arrian tells us (1.16.1), the Persians started to lose as they and their horses were being struck in the face with *xystoi*. From these passages we can see that the spear used by the Macedonian Companion Cavalry was the *xyston*, it was made from cornel-wood, and it was possible to fight with the rear end of it when it was broken in battle.

Marble funerary *lekythos* in Athens (National Museum 2586). The rider is heavily equipped with a Boeotian helmet, and a muscle-cuirass with shoulder-guards and groin-flaps. He would originally have held a spear in his left hand, the haft being painted in. (Hellenic National Archaeological Museum © Hellenic Ministry of Culture)

An example of a cavalry spear with a main and a subsidiary head is shown in this relief of a man standing in front of a horse, originally from Argos and now in Athens (National Museum 5153). The relief has been stylistically dated to the early 4th century, but it might be a little later. The spear is rather short, which may have been a method employed to fit it into the relief. (Author's photograph)

Bringing the cavalry up to strength

One thing that concerned Xenophon was the continuous inability of the *hipparchoi* to recruit the cavalry up to its establishment strength of 1,000. In the *Hipparchikos* (9.3–6), he proposed the engagement of 200 foreign mercenary cavalry, and we presume that this number would have made up the deficiency in recruiting. To defray the costs of providing their horses he suggested that money could be raised from those who strongly object to serving in the cavalry 'since even men actually enrolled on are willing to pay in order to get out of the service', from rich men who are physically unfit, and also from orphans possessed of large estates. He added his belief that some of the metics would be proud to be enrolled in the cavalry. He returned to the latter theme in *Revenues* (2.5), proposing once more that metics be admitted to the cavalry.

From a passage in the orator Deinarchus (*Against Demosthenes* 1.96), we can infer that Eubulus introduced measures for the improvement of the cavalry, although we are entirely ignorant of what these were. Eubulus, son of Spintharos was in control of Athenian finances from 354 to 350, shortly after Xenophon's *Revenues* was written. Perhaps these measures were financial, similar to those Xenophon recommended in his *Hipparchikos*. Nevertheless, when seven *phylai* of cavalry were sent out of Attica in 323 their strength amounted to only 500 men (Diodorus Siculus, *Hist.* 18.11.3).

THE ADMINISTRATION OF LYCURGUS

At the battle of Chaeronea in 338, Athens, in alliance with Thebes and other Greek states, was defeated by Philip II of Macedon. The Athenians lost 1,000 dead and 2,000 were taken prisoner, to be released shortly after. Athens, Thebes and other Greek states were forced into an alliance with Macedon. In the difficult position in which Athens found itself after the battle, Lycurgus, son of Lycophron, rose to prominence and played a major part in controlling the city's finances for a period of 12 years. He has been estimated to have raised state revenues to perhaps 1,200 talents per year. He held various offices, including steward of the military fund. It was probably during this period that generals were elected from the whole people, and not one per tribe.

State ownership of weapons

Athens being a democracy, it was the responsibility of every citizen to supply his own military equipment. Hoplite gear, of which the essential element was the hoplite shield, was very expensive. The only reliable price for a shield for the period, 20 drachmas, is known from an inscription dating to the early 3rd century from the island of Keos (*SIG*³ 958, 31). Throughout the 4th century we find that it was an increasingly common practice for wealthier citizens to donate to the state arms, and in particular shields, to enable their poorer fellow citizens to fight.

Pasion, who owned a shield factory, probably obtained citizenship by 386 thanks in part to his gift of 1,000 shields to the state (Demosthenes, *Against Stephanus* 45.85). An inscription from the *chalkothēkē*, the 'bronze store' (arsenal) on the Acropolis, dating to 369/68 lists 778 of them as still being in store (Davies 1971: 435). In the aftermath of the battle of Chaeronea, the Athenian general Charidemus gave shields to the state (Demosthenes, *On the Crown* 18.114).

Plutarch records (*Mor.* 852c) that Lycurgus, when in charge of military affairs, placed many sets of armour and 50,000 missiles in the Acropolis. Pausanias also reports (*Desc.* 1.29.16) that Lycurgus provided Athens with arms and missiles, not privately any more, but out of public funds. He was responsible for a variety of building programmes, civic and military, including the completion of a new arsenal (*skeuothēkē*) capable of accommodating the increased number of weapons that were in state ownership (Bertosa 2003).

Athenian catapults

Catapults were invented in Syracuse in 399. The word 'catapult' has nothing to do with the shield called a *peltē*; it is rather derived from the verb *katapallō* ('to strike down'), a compound of the Greek particles *kata-* and *pallō*. The first type of catapult was called a *gastraphetēs*, or 'stomach operated', because it required the full weight of the body to draw and cock it. It consisted of an extra-strong composite bow set crosswise on a base-frame, with a slide set on top of the frame to cock the bow. The bow itself was too strong to be pulled back by hand, but if the shooter placed the slide against the ground and pushed downwards towards the ground with his belly, with the bowstring attached to the frame, when the arms of the bow were fully tensed, the bowstring was secured by a trigger mechanism. A bolt much heavier, and with much more penetrative power than an arrow, could now be shot at the enemy.

The inscription (*IG* ii² 5426) on the architrave of this grave-monument (*naiskos*) in Athens (National Museum 738) proclaims it had been erected in memory of Aristonautes, son of Archenautes, from the deme of Halai. This is one of the latest in the series of extravagant funerary monuments in Athens before their banning under the administration of Demetrius of Phaleron (r. 317–307). He wears tunic and cloak; his muscle-cuirass is fitted with shoulder-guards, and with no fewer than three rows of groin-flaps. He wears a Phrygian helmet, but the cheek-pieces would have been bronze attachments to the marble statue now lost. Greaves were never worn by Athenian infantry during this period. (Author's photograph)

The date of the first inscription (*IG* ii² 1422, 9) referring to catapults at Athens is an inventory carried out of items stored in the *chalkothēkē* on the Acropolis mentioning 'two boxes of catapult bolts'. The date of this inscription is disputed: 371/70 and 363/62 have both been proposed. The gravestone of a catapult operator (*katapaltaphetas*), a Mysian called Herakleidas, has been discovered in the Piraeus dating to *c*.350–340 (*IG* ii² 9979). He was probably stationed at the fort of Mounychia where the *ephēboi* received part of their instruction. They may have been instructed in the use of the catapult even before the reform of the *ephēbeia* in 335.

The reform of the ephebate

The death of Philip and false rumours of Alexander's death caused the Thebans to renounce the Macedonian alliance in 335. In a lightning campaign Alexander threw himself against Thebes, destroyed it and sold its citizens into slavery. The effect on Athens was profound, and it may have been the main motive for reforming the *ephēbeia* that same year (Bertosa 2003: 374). According to Harpocration (s.v.), one Epicrates was responsible for a 'law concerning the *ephēbeia*'. The reformed system is described in chapter 42 of the *Athenaiōn Politeia*, which was written c.325.

The main effect of this decree was that, just as Xenophon had recommended, for the first time a subsistence payment (*trophē*) was introduced, enabling all to participate fully in the training: four obols for every *ephēbos* and a drachma (six obols) for the supervising staff – one *cosmētēs*, who was in charge of 'orderliness', and two *sōphronisai* in charge of 'self-control' who were elected from the citizens. These were not newly created offices. Demosthenes' *On The Embassy* (19.285), delivered in 343, refers to the two *sōphronisai*. The names of the *ephēboi* were no longer listed on whitewashed boards, but 'inscribed on a bronze pillar, and the pillar was set up in front of the council house near the statues of the tribal heroes' (*AP* 53.4).

The first year the *ephēboi* were stationed at two forts in the Piraeus, Mounichion and Akte, and taught by instructors (*didaskaloi*) in four skills: handling hoplite weapons, bows, javelins and catapults. We know that several of the instructors were foreigners, and so they must have received pay (*misthos*). The second year began with a parade in the theatre, at which the *ephēboi* demonstrated to the adult citizens what they had learnt, and they received a shield and a spear from the state. The second year was spent in patrolling the borders of the country. So, basically in the first year all were trained as hoplites, alongside the other skills that they learned, and the second year was spent patrolling out of the forts on the borders of Attica. The *Athēniaōn Politeia* tells us (42.5) that for the whole of the two years the *ephēboi* wore a *chlamys*, which was presumably black in colour, as previously discussed.

Arming of slaves in Athens

Athenaeus tells us (*Deip.* 6.272c) that Ctesicles, in the third book of his *Chronicles*, says that during the 117th Olympiad, at Athens a census was carried out by Demetrius of Phaleron of those dwelling in Attica. The number of (adult, male) Athenians was found to be 21,000; of metics, 10,000; and of slaves, 400,000. The figure for slaves may include both females and males. This high number of slaves is confirmed by a fragment of the orator Hypereides (frag. 18), which gives the number of slaves working in the mines and in the countryside (working in agriculture) as 150,000. After the Athenian defeat at Chaeronea, Hypereides moved that the slaves should be enfranchised and the metics granted Athenian citizenship (Lycurgus, *Against Leocrates* 41; Plutarch, *Mor.* 849a). In the panic the temples were stripped of the arms dedicated there (Lycurgus 44). Perhaps the aim was to arm the slaves, though no source directly states this.

Athenian demography

Following the reform of the *ephēbeia* in 335, it became the practice of the 19th year-group of each tribe to erect an inscription thanking their officers

Front and back views of a lead token, 20cm in diameter (after Kroll 1977: pl. 40,7). It was probably used in the armoury (*skeuothēkē*) in the agora to signify a shield that had been issued out. The obverse shows a shield bearing the letter *Alpha*, standing for 'The Athenians'. The reverse of the tokens bearing shields are all struck with the Greek letter 'A'. (Natalia Kozłowska)

on passing out of the institution (Friend 2019). These inscriptions include a list of the *ephēboi*, and notwithstanding the incompleteness of many of them, when we subtract the 'ephebic officers', the *taxiarchoi* and *lochagoi*, allow us to calculate the number of *ephēboi* passing out each year (i.e. in their 19th year) to have been *c*.466.

Figures for the total number of Athenian male citizens in the last half of the 4th century are given by five sources. Plato (*Critias* 112d–e), writing *c*.350, posits 20,000. Plutarch (*Mor.* 843d–e), writing *c*.338/37, tells us that Lycurgus brought Diphilos to trial for removing the rock supports from his mines. Diphilos was sentenced to death and his total estate of 160 talents was distributed, each citizen receiving 50 drachmas. If we do the arithmetic the figure is 19,200 for the total adult male population. Demosthenes informs us that 'there are about 20,000 of all us Athenians' (*Against Aristogien* 25.51). The passage of Athenaeus (*Deip.* 6.272c) preserving the information that there were 21,000 Athenians has already been mentioned.

One statistic remains. Following his victory in the Lamian War, Antipater imposed a new constitution on the Athenians, limiting the census and curbing the radical democracy. According to Diodorus Siculus (*Hist.* 18.18.4–5), those possessing less than 2,000 drachmas were excluded from voting and from public affairs. More than 22,000 lost their full citizenship while about 9,000 retained it. Thus, according to Diodorus Siculus' account, the total number of citizens in 322 would be more than 31,000. According to Plutarch (*Pho.* 28.4), however, the number of those deprived of their franchise was more than 12,000. Therefore, Plutarch would set the total population at more than 21,000. Given that the four other sources give a total citizen population of *c*.20,000, we should conclude that Diodorus Siculus is mistaken.

If we adopt an appropriate demographic life table, this gives a theoretical total of 8,535 males aged 20–39. Diodorus Siculus tells us (*Hist.* 18.10.2)

ATHENIAN FORCES IN THE LYCURGAN PERIOD

This plate tries to reconstruct the appearance of Athenian soldiers in the 330s and 320s.

(1) Hoplite

This figure is based on the grave-monument of Aristonautes. It seems that in the earlier representations of muscle-cuirasses on Athenian funerary sculpture they are not fitted with groin-flaps, but in the later ones they are. Xenophon recommends (*On Horsemanship* 12.4) that groin-flaps should be of such a material and size that they will keep out missiles. When closed, the cheek-flaps of the Phrygian helmet gave almost complete protection to the facial area.

(2) Catapult instructor

The *gastraphetēs* continued to be used alongside more powerful and sophisticated models developed during the course of the later 4th century. It was only after the *gastraphetēs* was returned to a horizontal position that a bolt (not shown) could be placed on the slider.

(3) Impressed man

This figure seeks to reconstruct the appearance of a poor man unable to equip himself with arms and armour, who is issued by the Athenian state with a shield and spear. The shield bears the letter 'A', standing for 'The Athenians'.

We only have evidence for shields decorated with the letter *Alpha* from the Hellenistic period. Nevertheless, with the accumulating number of hoplite shields under state ownership

stored in the *chalkothēkē* on the Acropolis, and later in the *skeuothēkē* in the agora, the idea must have arisen to mark them in some way. We have already seen that shields of a standard, reduced weight produced for the *hoplitodromos* would have been stored alongside these shields in the armouries, some at least decorated with the letters 'AΘH' or 'A'. The idea of marking these shields with the letter 'A' must surely have come from these sporting shields among which they were stored.

American excavations in the Athenian Agora discovered a dump of lead tokens in a well some 70m away from the site of the Athenian *skeuothēkē* in the agora (Kroll 1977). These lead tokens show on one side an item of armour, such as a helmet or a cuirass, and on the reverse the letters A, B, Γ and Δ, which Kroll interpreted as standing for its size (no example of a reverse stamped with the letter 'B' has survived). Other, related material has been gathered by Schäfer (2019). A number of these tokens show hoplite shields with the letter 'A' as a blazon. Though these tokens seem to be early Hellenistic in date rather than late Classical, the same shield blazon could well have been in use earlier on.

The only literary evidence we have concerning Athenian shield decoration during this period is Plutarch's statement (*Dem.* 20.2) that at the battle of Chaeronea, Demosthenes had 'Good Luck!' written on his shield in gold. We are not told whether the words were written on the inside of the shield, or on the rim, or alongside a blazon.

A 'naval battle in the Hellespont' is mentioned in one inscription (*IG* ii² 398) and the Athenian fallen 'at Abydus' in another (*IG* ii² 493). Both of these inscriptions seem to refer to the same incident, which took place during the Lamian War. This gravestone in Munich (GL 522) in memory of Demetrius son of Alexeas was found east of Cyzicus on the southern shore of the Hellespont. It could be Attic in style and script, and Demetrius has been tentatively associated with an Athenian naval hoplite who fell in that battle. (Bibi Saint-Pol/Wikimedia/Public Domain)

that in 323 the Athenians decided to call up all men up to the age of 40, that three tribal regiments should defend Attica, and seven should be ready to campaign outside the borders. Later (18.11.3) he says this latter force consisted of 5,000 citizen infantry, 500 citizen cavalry and 2,000 mercenaries. Ten sevenths of 5,500 gives a total of 7,857 men for all the ten tribes, a statistical shortfall of 678, or 8 per cent from the expected total. The confirmation of the universal liability for military service could not be more evident. (I present the evidence fully in Sekunda 1992.) Hansen (1994) argues against the evidence presented above point by point, believing that the male adult citizen population of Athens was about 30,000 in the 4th century, and the same, according to Herodotus (*Hist.* 5.97), as during the 5th century. This causes considerable difficulties; apart from Athens not having lost any manpower during the Peloponnesian War, it makes military training in the *ephēbeia* and indeed military service as a whole voluntary, which was plainly not the case.

Athens never recovered from the military defeat it suffered during the Lamian War and the constitution imposed on it by Antipater. Athenian forces were defeated on land at Crannon in Thessaly, and at sea in three battles at Amorgos, Abydus and the Echinades islands. Both the Athenian army and the navy ceased to be forces to be reckoned with.

The 'Mourning Athena' preserved in the Acropolis Museum (695), dated to c.460 on stylistic grounds, symbolizes the collective state mourning enforced at Athens. We do not know at what point the Athenians started to bury their war dead collectively. The earliest securely dated casualty list is from 464 (*IG* i³ 464; Low 2010: 341 n.3). Here, Athena reads the list of the fallen of the city of which she was patron. (Harrieta171/Wikimedia/ CC BY-SA 3.0)

BIBLIOGRAPHY

Alexandri, Olga (1973). Ἡρανός «βοιωτιουργὲς» εξ Ἀθηνων', *Arch. Eph.* 1973: 93–105, pls. 51–54.

Barley, Nick (2015). 'Aeneas Tacticus and Small Units in Greek Warfare' in Geoff Lee, Helene Whittaker & Graham Wrightson, eds, *Ancient Warfare: Introducing Current Research, Volume I.* Newcastle upon Tyne: Cambridge Scholars Publishing: pp. 43–64.

Beazley, J.D. (1963). *Attic Red-Figure Vase-Painters.* 2nd Edition. Oxford: Oxford University Press.

Bertosa, Brian (2003). 'The Supply of Hoplite Equipment by the Athenian State Down to the Lamian War', *The Journal of Military History* 67: 361–79.

Billigmeier, Jon-Christian & Dusing, Kathleen Ann Sutherland (1981). 'The origin and function of the *naukraroi* at Athens: an etymological and historical explanation', *Transactions of the American Philological Association* 111: 11–16.

Bugh, Glenn Richard (1988). *The Horsemen of Athens.* Princeton, NJ: Princeton University Press.

Christ, Matthew R. (2001). 'Conscription of Hoplites in Classical Athens', *Classical Quarterly* 51: 398–422.

Crowley, Jason (2012). *The Psychology of the Athenian Hoplite: The Culture of Combat in Classical Athens.* Cambridge: Cambridge University Press.

Davies, J.K. (1971). *Athenian Propertied Families, 600–300 B.C.* Oxford: Clarendon Press.

Everson, Tim (2004). *Warfare in Ancient Greece: Arms and Armour From the Heroes of Homer to Alexander the Great.* Thrupp: Sutton Publishing.

Fornara, Charles W. (1977). *Translated Documents of Greece and Rome, Volume One: Archaic Times to the End of the Peloponnesian War.* Baltimore, MD: The Johns Hopkins University Press.

Friend, John L. (2019). *The Athenian Ephebeia in the Fourth Century BCE.* Leiden: Brill.

Hansen, H.H. (1994). 'The Number of Athenian Citizens *secundum* Sekunda', *Échos du Monde Classique* 13: 299–310.

Harding, Philip (1985). *Translated Documents of Greece and Rome, Volume Two: From the End of the Peloponnesian War to the Battle of Ipsus.* Cambridge: Cambridge University Press.

Hignett, C. (1952). *A History of the Athenian Constitution.* Oxford: Clarendon Press.

Kroll, John H. (1977). 'Some Athenian Armour Tokens', *Hesperia* 46: 141–46, pl. 40.

Low, Polly (2010). 'Commemoration of the war dead in classical Athens: remembering defeat and victory', in David M. Pritchard, *War, Democracy and Culture in Classical Athens.* Cambridge: Cambridge University Press: pp. 341–58.

Martin, Albert (1887). *Les cavaliers athéniens.* Paris: E. Thorin.

Meritt, Benjamin D. (1984). 'The Saddle-Cloths of Alkibiades', in Harold D. Evjen, ed., *Mnemai: Classical Studies in Memory of Karl K. Hulley.* Chisinau: Scholars Press: pp. 93–96.

Murray, Sarah C. (2022). *Male Nudity in the Greek Iron Age: Representation and ritual context in Aegean societies.* Cambridge: Cambridge University Press.

Monument to the Ten Eponymous Heroes in the Athenian agora. The Athenian heroes from which the ten Athenian tribes took their names were each represented by a bronze statue, below which official notices relevant to the tribe were posted. (Author's photograph)

Raubitschek, A. (1956). 'The Gates in the Agora', *American Journal of Archaeology* 60: 279–82.

Robertson, Martin & Frantz, Alison (1975). *The Parthenon Frieze*. Oxford: Oxford University Press.

Schäfer, Martin (2019). 'The Armour Token from the Athenian Agora', in Antonino Crisà, Mairi Gkikaki & Clare Rowan, eds, *Tokens: Culture, Connections, Communities*. Royal Numismatic Society Special Publication No. 57: pp. 41–61.

Sekunda, N.V. (1990). '*IG* ii² 1250: A Decree Concerning the *Lampadephoroi* of the Tribe Aiantis', *Zeitschrift für Papyrologie und Epigraphik* 83: 149–82, pl. IV.

Sekunda, N.V. (1992). 'Athenian Demography and Military Strength 338–322 B.C.', *Annual of the British School at Athens* 87: 311–55.

Sekunda, Nicholas (2016). 'The Mounted Torch-Race at the Athenian Bendideia', in Krzysztof Ulanowski, ed., *The Religious Aspects of War in the Ancient Near East, Greece and Rome*. Leiden: Brill: pp. 206–34.

Sekunda, Nick & McBride, Angus (1986). *The Ancient Greeks*. Elite 7. London: Osprey Publishing.

Sparkes, Brian A. (1977). 'Quintain and the Talcott Class', *Antike Kunst* 20: 8–25.

Spence, I.G. (1987). 'Athenian Cavalry Numbers in the Peloponnesian War: *IG* i³ 375 Revisited', *Zeitschrift für Papyrologie und Epigraphik* 110: 167–75.

Spence, I.G. (1990). 'Perikles and the Defence of Attika during the Peloponnesian War', *Journal of Hellenic Studies* 110: 91–109.

Spence, I.G. (1993). *The Cavalry of Classical Greece: A Social and Military History with Particular Reference to Athens*. Oxford: Clarendon Press.

Stevenson, Tom (2003). 'Cavalry Uniforms on the Parthenon Frieze?', *American Journal of Archaeology* 107: 629–54.

Trendall, A.D. & Cambitoglou, Alexander (1982). *The Red-Figured Vases of Apulia, Vol. II: Late Apulian*. Oxford: Clarendon Press.

Trundle, Matthew (2010). 'Light Troops in Classical Athens', in David M. Pritchard, ed., *War, Democracy and Culture in Classical Athens*. Cambridge: Cambridge University Press: pp. 139–60.

Van Wees, Hans (2013). *Ships and Silver, Taxes and Tribute: A Fiscal History of Archaic Athens*. London: I.B. Tauris.

INDEX

References to illustrations are shown in **bold**.
Plates are shown with page locators in brackets.